A LOOK at the OLD TESTAMENT

An Abridged Survey of Genesis—Malachi

By Henrietta C. Mears

G/L REGAL BOOKS

A Division of G/L Publications
Glendale, California, U.S.A.

Over 100,000 in print

Second Printing, 1967
Third Printing, 1968
Fourth Printing, 1969
Fifth Printing, 1970
Sixth Printing, 1972

© Copyright 1966 by G/L Publications

Printed in U.S.A.

Published by
Regal Books Division, G/L Publications
Glendale, California 91209, U.S.A.

ISBN 0-8307-0009-9

A STRING OF PEARLS

"Most people's knowledge of history is like a string of graduated pearls without the string," said an historian.

This statement seems to be especially true of Bible history. Many people know the Bible characters and the principal events, but they are hopelessly lost when they are called upon to connect the stories in order. Anyone who has experienced the thrill of learning to place the individual characters in their right setting as to place and time can realize the difference it makes in his enjoyment of God's Word.

This book will enable you to pick up the "pearls" in the Scriptures and string them in order, from Genesis to Malachi.

You will find this volume and its companion, *A Look at the New Testament,* to be admirably suited as study guides. They are in fact abridgments of a more comprehensive volume, *What the Bible Is All About,* which has proved an excellent teaching tool for instructors of Bible study groups.

INTRODUCTION

Have you ever climbed a very high mountain and upon arriving at the summit were thrilled with the breath-taking view? While traveling through the valleys you had seen the details — the tree, the flower, the brook and the stone. But from the mountaintop you had a panoramic view of the vast expanses of God's wonderful nature. This survey of the Bible is planned to give you such a panoramic view of the inspired Word of God, the Holy Bible. From this viewpoint you will see it as a cohesive whole instead of as a series of unrelated stories or details.

The Bible is the story of what God is doing in history. Like any good story, it has a beginning and an ending. It starts with the creation; conflict is introduced with the workings of Satan and the fall of man, introducing the dilemma. The rest of the story is the solving of that grand dilemma by God, and the final triumph of His purpose at the second coming of Christ. All the events in between fit into that story and contribute to the unfolding of the "plot." The Bible has one main theme — redemption — and many sub-themes which run through the entire book. Redemption is hinted at in the beginning — Genesis 3:15 — and developed as the main subject, coming to a climax with the advent of Christ. The sub-themes, interwoven into the narrative, and all dependent upon the main theme, redemption, are defined and illustrated in the events of the Bible.

Along with this panoramic view of the Bible goes the *specific* lesson to be found in each book. Of course, there are nearly as many lessons to be drawn as there are verses; but rather than doing that kind of detailed study, this volume aims to give an inclusive picture of the Bible and the general lessons to be drawn from each book.

Fortunately, the twentieth-century thirst for knowledge includes in America a wholesome curiosity about what the Bible teaches. In accompaniment to churches' expanding Sunday school enrollments, home Bible-study groups are springing up and churches gladly respond to desires for weekday classes.

Such groups find this volume and its companion, *A Look at the New Testament,* to be admirably suited for study guides. They are in fact abridgments of a parent volume, *What the Bible Is All About,* which has proved an excellent teaching tool for instructors.

In reading the book now in your hand remember that it is a wonderful privilege to have and to hold the precious Word of God. People of other days have been denied this privilege. Even now, in some nations, the Bible is a forbidden book and the public teaching of it is considered a crime against the state. In pagan lands millions have never had the opportunity of hearing its message or reading its pages. It is therefore not only your privilege but also your sacred responsibility to study the Scriptures. You will find *A Look at the Old Testament* a great aid in this essential study. Accept this privilege and responsibility seriously. Carefully follow the directions found in this book. Become acquainted with the characters portrayed in God's holy revelation.

The daily Bible readings will lead you step by step into an understanding of the sixty-six books of Holy Scripture. Check the progress you are making by using the review questions found at the end of each section of your book. As you conscientiously use this *A Look at the Old Testament,* you will find yourself becoming *approved unto God, a workman that needeth not to be ashamed, rightly dividing the word of truth* (II Timothy 2:15).

CONTENTS

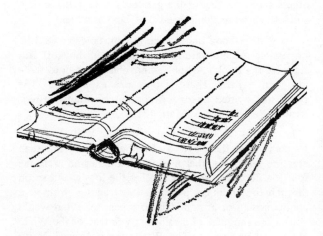

Chapter 1

LET'S LOOK AT THE BIBLE

THE BIBLE PORTRAYS JESUS CHRIST,
THE SAVIOUR OF THE WORLD

THE AUTHORS

Seldom has any book had the name of more than one or two authors. But the Bible was written by forty authors, covering a period of sixteen hundred years. Moses commenced it in the desert of Arabia and John completed it on the isle of Patmos. This would make it impossible for them to have any understanding as to what the purpose of the book would be or what part they should write.

The authors were poets and philosophers, sages and

singers, princes and kings, fishermen and statesmen. Some were learned in all the arts of the Egyptians, others sat at the feet of the greatest scholars of the day, still others were "unlearned and ignorant men."

To write a book under such circumstances would be impossible if there were to be any unity in thought! But we have the Book. A Book impossible for men to write has been written. There is only one explanation. The Book was written by one Author, using many writers. Read II Peter 1:21; see Mark 13:31.

Is not this all a proof that it was not written merely by men? Was there ever a cathedral built, by one man erecting a wall, another a window, another an arch, the fourth a doorway, and yet another the tower, and so on through the countless parts of the structure, without a common plan or an architect to supervise? What would you say to the man who said that was true of the White House at Washington, or Westminster Abbey? If we cannot believe this of a monument of mortar and stone, what about this grander cathedral of truth built through greater periods of time? Could its unity be a mere accident?

Although few of the writers of the Bible were of sufficient scholarship to write a book, nevertheless each wrote a book which perfectly fits into the other sixty-five books of the Bible. Why was this true? *For the prophecy came not in old time by the will of man: but holy men of God spake as they were moved by the Holy Ghost* (II Peter 1:21).

Men do not send their writings to the printer without careful rewriting and revision. But no Bible writer revised his work. Moses did not discover he had left out valuable information from Genesis. God saw to that! Nothing new has ever been discovered during the centuries since the Bible has been written that needs to be added to the Word or in any way brings disrepute on

2

BIBLE LANDS

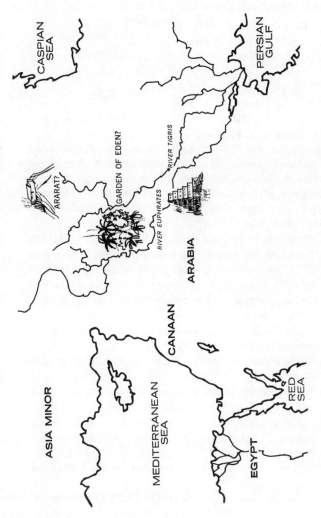

CASPIAN SEA

PERSIAN GULF

ARARAT?

GARDEN OF EDEN?

RIVER TIGRIS

RIVER EUPHRATES

ARABIA

ASIA MINOR

CANAAN

MEDITERRANEAN SEA

RED SEA

EGYPT

it. Only of the Bible, God's Book, can it be said, and God Himself must say it, *Ye shall not add unto the word which I command you, neither shall ye diminish ought from it* (Deut. 4:2).

BIBLE DIVISIONS

Old Testament	New Testament
5 Law	4 Gospels
12 Historical	
5 Poetical	Acts
17 Prophetical	21 Epistles
(5 Major)	
(12 Minor)	Revelation

INTERESTING FACTS

The word "Bible" comes from the Greek word "biblos," meaning "book." Christ called it "The Scriptures" (John 5:39; Matt. 22:29). Paul called it the "Word of God" or the "Holy Scriptures" (Romans 1:2). It is also called "the law and the prophets" (Luke 16:16).

The word "Testament" means "covenant." In the Old Testament we have the covenant God made with man about his salvation *before* Christ came. In the New Testament we have the *covenant of grace* which is God's agreement with man about his salvation *after* Christ came.

The Old Testament is nearly three and a half times as large as the New.

The Historical books cover over one-half of the Old Testament.

The Poetical books about one-fifth of the Old Testament.

The Pentateuch (the first five books of the Bible, written by Moses) is almost as large as the New Testament.

The Gospels are almost one-half of the New Testament.

The Old Testament was written mostly in Hebrew.

The New Testament was written wholly in Greek.

The deathless Book has survived three great dangers: the negligence of its friends; the false systems built upon it; the warfare of those who have hated it.

The Bible expounds the perfect will of God, the sinful condition of man, the wonderful plan of salvation. Its law is perfect, its teachings binding, its records are true.

Read it to be wise.
Believe it to be safe.
Practice it to be holy.

Read the Bible slowly, frequently, and prayerfully. It is a book you are to live by. It is a book out of which you are to be judged. It demands the highest consideration and will reward the earnest student.

HISTORICAL ACCURACY

We find ancient histories filled with many misstatements. Not so with the Bible. But a few years back the story of Joseph and the seven years of famine was pronounced a myth by historians. The idea of the Nile not overflowing its banks for seven years was inconceivable to them. The author once had the pleasure of visiting the tombs of the kings in Upper Egypt and seeing what the spade of the archaeologist has discovered. Tablets and monuments, upon which we find stories recorded to the last and least detail, line the walls of these sepulchres which have been hidden for centuries.

Five thousand places mentioned in the Bible have been definitely located by geographers and explorers. Perfectly marvelous confirmations have been worked out. Sir Charles Marston has given us many of these facts.

The deeper the archaeological spade goes down, the higher Biblical chronology and history go up. God is keeping a record of this for us.

ARCHAEOLOGICAL EVIDENCE

The very stones cry out in confirmation of the Word.

Some have thought that Nabonidus and not Belshazzar was king at the time of the destruction of Babylon (Daniel 5:1,30). The report was that Belshazzar was neither captured nor killed but escaped at a battle outside the capital. He was beaten, taken prisoner and then became governor under the conqueror, living in luxury and dying in peace.

Hence Belshazzar was read out of the Bible. But over twenty-five years ago from the mounds that mark the almost forgotten site of that once great city of Babylon, a cylinder, inscribed with curious records, was taken, telling us that Belshazzar was the son of Nabonidus and was regent under him, sharing the throne of his father. He was slain at Babylon while his father escaped and survived. Out of the ruins of buried cities rises a new witness to the Word. Never fear the truth of the Bible record.

ONE BOOK, ONE HISTORY, ONE STORY

The Bible is one book, one story—His-story. When you look carefully through it, you find one great purpose. It is this, God is redeeming a sinful world. Don't suppose that reading little scraps of this great revelation of God will ever give you an idea of the wonders of the Word.

> "I supposed I knew my Bible,
> Reading piecemeal, hit or miss,
> Now a bit of John or Matthew,
> Now a snatch of Genesis;
> Certain chapters of Isaiah,
> Certain Psalms (the twenty-third!)
> Twelfth of Romans, First of Proverbs,
> Yes, I thought I knew the Word!
> But I found that thorough reading
> Was a different thing to do
> And the way was unfamiliar
> When I read the Bible through.

"You who like to play at Bible,
Dip and dabble, here and there,
Just before you kneel, aweary,
And yawn through a hurried prayer,
You who treat the Crown of Writings
As you treat no other book—
Just a paragraph disjointed,
Just a crude, impatient look—
Try a worthier procedure,
Try a broad and steady view;
You will kneel in very rapture
When you read the Bible through!"

THE BIBLE SPEAKS FOR ITSELF

*The law of the LORD is perfect, converting the soul:
the testimony of the LORD is sure, making wise the
simple. The statutes of the Lord are right, rejoicing the
heart: the commandment of the Lord is pure, enlight-
ening the eyes* (Psalm 19:7,8).

*Wherewithal shall a young man cleanse his way? by
taking heed thereto according to thy word* (Psalm
119:9).

*And that from a child thou hast known the holy
scriptures, which are able to make thee wise unto
salvation through faith which is in Christ Jesus* (II
Timothy 3:15).

*All scripture is given by inspiration of God, and is
profitable for doctrine, for reproof, for correction, for
instruction in righteousness: that the man of God may
be perfect, throughly furnished unto all good works* (II
Timothy 3:16,17).

*For the word of God is quick, and powerful, and
sharper than any two-edged sword* (Hebrews 4:12).

*For the prophecy came not in old time by the will of
man: but holy men of God spake as they were moved
by the Holy Ghost* (II Peter 1:21).

GREAT TESTIMONIES

George Washington

"It is impossible to rightly govern the world without God and the Bible."

Abraham Lincoln

"I believe the Bible is the best gift God has ever given to man. All the good from the Saviour of the world is communicated to us through this Book."

Napoleon

"The Bible is no mere book, but a Living Creature with a power that conquers all that oppose it."

CORDS THAT BIND THE BIBLE TOGETHER
Black thread of Ruin—The Fall.
Scarlet thread of Redemption—Blood of Christ.
Golden thread of Regeneration—Spirit of God.

The Old Testament, like the cordage of the British Navy, has the scarlet thread of sacrifice (the blood) running through it. The scarlet cord was completed at Calvary when Jesus Christ shed His precious blood.

Minimum Daily Requirements / Spiritual Vitamins

Sunday: GOD-GIVEN II Timothy 3:10-17
Monday: SHOULD BE TREASURED Deut. 11:1-9; Josh. 1:8,9
Tuesday: SHOULD BE KEPT Psalm 119:9-18
Wednesday: A LAMP Psalm 119:105-117
Thursday: FOOD Isaiah 55:1-11; Matt. 4:4
Friday: FULFILLED Luke 24:36-45
Saturday: COMPLETE Revelation 22:8-21

Chapter 2

LET'S LOOK AT GENESIS

GENESIS PORTRAYS JESUS CHRIST,
OUR CREATOR GOD

A BOOK OF BEGINNINGS

The Book of Genesis is a book of important beginnings. It tells the beginning of everything but God. The key verse is Genesis 1:1.

Genesis begins with "God" but ends "in a coffin." (Genesis 1:1; 50:26) This book is a history of man's failure. But we find that God meets every failure of man. He is a glorious Saviour.

9

In many respects Genesis is the most important book in the Bible. It is the seed plot of the whole Book. Every great fact and truth is found here in germ. It is the foundation on which God builds the entire revelation of truth. If you start right as you read God's Word, you proceed in the right direction. If you get off the track here, you find yourself floundering all through the Book.

WHO WROTE GENESIS?

The age long Hebrew and Christian position is that Moses, guided by the Spirit of God, wrote Genesis. The book ends three hundred years before Moses was born. Moses could have received his information only by direct revelation from God or from historical records to which he had access, that had been handed down from his forefathers. (Amos 3:7) See what Jesus said about Moses. (Luke 24:27; John 7:19)

GENESIS IS THE BOOK OF BEGINNINGS

1. The beginning of the world, Genesis 1:1-25
2. The beginning of the human race, Genesis 1:26–2
3. The beginning of sin in the world, Genesis 3:1-7
4. The beginning of the promise of redemption, Genesis 3:8-24
5. The beginning of family life, Genesis 4:1-15
6. The beginning of a man-made civilization, Genesis 4:16–9:29
7. The beginning of the nations of the world, Genesis 10; 11
8. The beginning of the Hebrew race, Genesis 12–50

EGYPT, CANAAN
SINAI PENINSULA

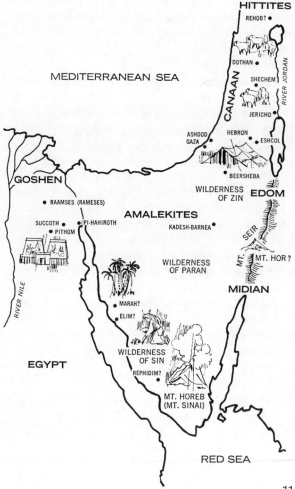

HITTITES

REHOB?

MEDITERRANEAN SEA

DOTHAN

SHECHEM

RIVER JORDAN

CANAAN

JERICHO

ASHDOD
GAZA

HEBRON

ESHCOL

GOSHEN

BEERSHEBA

RAAMSES (RAMESES)

WILDERNESS
OF ZIN

EDOM

SUCCOTH
PITHOM

PI-HAHIROTH

AMALEKITES

KADESH-BARNEA

SEIR

RIVER NILE

WILDERNESS
OF PARAN

MT.

MT. HOR?

MIDIAN

MARAH?

ELIM?

WILDERNESS
OF SIN

EGYPT

REPHIDIM?

MT. HOREB
(MT. SINAI)

RED SEA

11

CREATION (Genesis 1; 2)

As the curtain rises, we hear a voice. It is the voice of God. For in the beginning God was there. God spoke and worlds were framed by His word. (Hebrews 11:3)

God created this universe for His glory. Then God created man in His image that he might have companionship with Him and placed him in the Garden of Eden.

Genesis tells us that:

The Lord our God is one Lord. (Deut. 6:4; Mark 12:29)

God is the Creator of this universe. (Genesis 1; 2)

God existed before all things. (Genesis 1:1)

The wonderful truth is that God created man that He might have fellowship with him. Imagine, the great God who created all things wants to have fellowship with us. Are you having it? Do you spend time each day with the Lord who made you for Himself?

For further study find all the references you can in the Scriptures (1) to creation, and (2) to Adam, the chief human character of this first scene. You will find some in the New Testament as well as the Old.

What answer would you be able to give from your knowledge of Genesis as to the creation of this universe and man? Be prepared to make a statement because you will constantly be confronted with this question.

THE FALL (Genesis 3; 4)

As this scene opens we see Adam and Eve in the beautiful Garden of Eden. Satan, the author of sin, acting through a serpent, enters the garden and begins his sinister role as the subtle tempter of mankind. Through him man doubted God's Word and even His authority and goodness. Adam and Eve yielded to the temptation and sin entered the world.

As the scene closes we see man driven from the presence of God. Sorrow filled his heart. The ground was cursed and all nature suffered. We see God's grace even in this act by which sin entered the world. God in His mercy promised One who would redeem man from sin. (Genesis 3:15) Jesus, the seed of woman, will come as our Redeemer. Satan shall bruise His heel (He will give His life as a payment for our sins) but He (Christ) shall bruise his head. Yes, Christ shall deal a deadly blow to the adversary and destroy his works. Christ will be the Triumphant One.

What breaks our fellowship with God? Sin. Sin is anything that separates you from God or from your fellow men. What will you do then? (I John 1:9)

Can you account for the presence of sin in the world today?

THE FLOOD (Genesis 5–9)

As the curtain rises again in Genesis 5, we see the world in a state of awful wickedness. (Read Genesis 6:5.) It increased so that only one righteous man was left, Noah. God's patience was most wonderful, but because His mercies were refused, God sent a flood to cover the earth.

Noah was saved from the flood by the ark. If we only will accept it, God always makes a way of escape from judgment in His Son who is our Ark of safety. Just as there was only one ark for a way of escape in the day of Noah, so there is only one Saviour who offers salvation. (Acts 4:12; John 14:6)

Have you accepted the Lord Jesus Christ as your Saviour, and are you safe in this insecure day in the Ark of safety? (Read John 1:12.)

People are always disturbed by the fact that the ark could not possibly carry the animals that God said should go into the ark. Do you know how to answer this question? What were the dimensions of that large ship? A cubit is approximately eighteen inches, the distance from the elbow to the tip of the middle finger. Figure out the dimensions of the ark. (Genesis 6:14-16)

The building of this huge vessel must have been a great object lesson to a wicked people. They had defied and sneered at God and His precepts. Now they were overwhelmed in their sins. We learn that though evil seems to be triumphant and carry all before it, yet in the end shall it be cut off.

God gave us the promise of a Redeemer in Genesis 3, and after this great flood God gave Noah the rainbow as a promise that never again would the earth be destroyed by water. With what will it be destroyed the next time? (II Peter 3:7)

THE SPADE UNEARTHS EVIDENCE OF FLOOD

New York, March 16, 1936—The Biblical story of the flood has the support of material evidence unearthed by science.

Sir Charles Marston has been called a decipherer of ancient clues. He outranks all the great detectives of modern fiction. He has unearthed thousands of witnesses in stone and pottery. He brings to light the truth concerning the Scriptures wherever he wields his spade. Sir Charles is called an "archaeologist with a purpose." His chief concern is to correct the critics of the Bible. Records of many persons that scientists have said never existed have been brought to light; many places that they said were only Bible names have been unearthed.

He tells us that beneath the surface, excavations reveal the remains of a vast civilization, reaching back more than five thousand years before the time of Christ.

The archaeological discoveries in Mesopotamia, to which attention has been drawn, give evidence of the flood, both in the cuneiform writings and in the actual flood deposits.

BABEL (Genesis 10; 11)

Now our scene is laid in the plain of Shinar. We see the sons of Noah building a great tower for themselves in defiance of God. They sought to establish a world-wide empire that would be independent of God. For this reason God sent a confusion of tongues and scattered them in many different lands. Then, in the providence of God, there arose tribes, nations and different languages according to the sons of Noah.

Sons of Shem settled in the east and China.

Sons of Ham settled in Africa.

Sons of Japheth settled in Europe.

How can you account for the different languages on the earth today? What Scripture can you give to verify your statement? (See chapter 11.)

THE CALL OF ABRAHAM (Genesis 12-38)

The scene is shifted from the plain of Shinar in Arabia to Ur of the Chaldees, an idolatrous but wonderful ancient city. The author had the privilege of standing in this city a few years ago. Today there is nothing left of this vast civilization but a pile of bricks and the great mound upon which the offerings to the sun god were made, which speak of former glory and grandeur.

As we listen, we hear God calling a man by the name of Abraham to leave his home and follow Him. God promised to make of him a great nation and offered him a great land. (Gen. 12:1-3)

Abraham obeyed and God made him the father of His chosen people, the Israelites (or Jews as they are commonly called today).

God renewed His covenant with Isaac (Abraham's son of promise) and then with Jacob who succeeded his father in the covenant relationship with God. His name was changed to Israel, meaning a "prince with God," because of his power in prayer. (Read the thrilling episode in Genesis 32:24-28.) This is where the name of God's chosen people originated, Israelites.

DESCENT INTO EGYPT (Genesis 39–50)

The last scene in the Book of Genesis is laid in Egypt. God permitted Joseph to be sold into Egypt by his envious brothers in order that these same brothers might follow him to find food in the time of famine. Joseph had been exalted to a place of rulership and so his brothers were royally received.

Egypt afforded the best civilization of that day, and no more pleasant home could be found than Goshen, near the Nile River.

God wanted to keep His people away from the corrupting influences of the Canaanites until they could be prepared for their mission. God wanted them to become His witnesses on the earth and from this chosen people was to come the Messiah, according to the flesh.

Read Jacob's dying words to his twelve sons. (Genesis 49) We see here again the promise of Shiloh who is to be the coming ruler. Remember, Christ is called the *Lion of the tribe of Judah* (Rev. 5:5).

The Book of Genesis ends in failure. The last words are "in a coffin in Egypt." Only death marks the pathway of sin; "the wages of sin is death." The people needed a Saviour!

There are eight names mentioned in Genesis that we should remember in sequence. Tell the story of Genesis by beginning with the first and finishing with the last.

God, Adam, Satan, Noah, Abraham, Isaac, Jacob, Joseph.

There are six places of supreme importance in connection with the history of Genesis—Eden, Mount

Ararat, Babel, Ur of the Chaldees, Canaan (the promised land), and Egypt.

AN IMPORTANT LESSON

THE BIBLE portrays Jesus Christ, the Saviour of the World.

GENESIS portrays Jesus Christ, Our Creator God.

EXODUS portrays Jesus Christ, Our Passover Lamb.

LEVITICUS portrays Jesus Christ, Our Sacrifice for Sin.

NUMBERS portrays Jesus Christ, Our "Lifted-Up One."

DEUTERONOMY portrays Jesus Christ, Our True Prophet.

JOSHUA portrays Jesus Christ, Captain of Our Salvation.

JUDGES portrays Jesus Christ, Our Deliverer Judge.

RUTH portrays Jesus Christ, Our Kinsman Redeemer.

I AND II SAMUEL portray Jesus Christ, Our King.

KINGS AND CHRONICLES portray Jesus Christ as King.

EZRA AND NEHEMIAH portray Jesus Christ, Our Restorer.

INFORMATION PLEASE

1. Does the Bible say that the world was created 6,000 years ago? (Genesis 1:1)

2. Was the world dark before the sun was created? (Genesis 1:3,4)

3. Which was first, morning or evening? (Genesis 1:5)

4. Where did Cain get his wife? (Genesis 3:20; 5:4)

5. How did the writer of Genesis know what happened on the earth before man appeared? (Acts 7:37-38; II Peter 1:21)

6. Where is the Garden of Eden located? (Genesis 2:8-14)

7. Will there ever be another flood? (Genesis 9:13-15)

Minimum Daily Requirements / Spiritual Vitamins

Sunday: CREATION Genesis 1:1-5; 26–31; 2:7-22

Monday: FALL Genesis 3: 1-24

Tuesday: DELUGE Gen. 6:1-7; 7:7-24; 8:6-11; 18–22; 9:1-16

Wednesday: BEGINNING OF LANGUAGES Genesis 11:1-9

Thursday: THE ABRAHAMIC CALL AND COVENANT Gen. 12:1-9; 13:14-18; 15:1-21; 17:4-8; 22:15-20; 26:1-5; 28:10-15

Friday: STORY OF JOSEPH Genesis 37:1-36; 42

Saturday: JACOB'S FINAL BLESSING Genesis 49

Chapter 3

LET'S LOOK AT EXODUS

*EXODUS PORTRAYS JESUS CHRIST,
OUR PASSOVER LAMB*

Exodus means "going out." It is the continuation of the first book, Genesis, which means "beginning." Genesis closes with the children of Israel in Egypt. As the curtain rises in Exodus, we see them still there.

TYPES OF CHRIST

Passover Lamb—Exodus 12:6; I Cor. 5:7,8.

Living Bread—Exodus 16:4; John 6:48-51.

The Smitten Rock—Exodus 17:6; I Cor. 10:4; John 4:13,14.

The Tabernacle—Exodus 29:42-46; Hebrews 8:5; 9:11.

The Great High Priest—Exodus 28:41; Lev. 21:10; Hebrews 7:23-28; 9:11.

THE BONDAGE (Exodus 1:1–22)

As we look into the great story in Exodus 1:7, we find that the Israelites had increased exceedingly. At the time of the Exodus there were 600,000 men (Exodus 12:37), which would average three million persons, including women and children. For seventy souls to reach this number in four hundred and thirty years is astounding. It meant that they composed almost half of Egypt's population. No wonder this gave the Egyptians a growing alarm. This is why the unfriendly Pharaohs sought to prevent further increase of population by severe oppression. (Exodus 1:8-14)

We see the hand of Satan working in this time of bondage. Pharaoh made a decree that all male Hebrew children should be destroyed. Satan was determined that the "Seed" promised to Abraham (the Messiah Christ) should not be born, for it was through this line that our Redeemer was to come.

This is the reason that God took Israel out of Canaan and placed them in Egypt so that they might become numerically strong. He wanted to protect them against the idolatry of the Canaanites in Palestine, for Israel must worship one true God, Jehovah.

We wonder why God allowed His chosen people to become slaves in Egypt, but He had a plan in it all. He wanted them to return to the promised land and become the channel through which He could work His plan of redemption. If they had been left in peace and plenty in Goshen, down in Egypt, they would never have wanted to leave their happy state. Often God allows trials to come so that we might be willing to leave one place and go where He wishes us.

In Exodus 1:11 we are told that the Israelites, while they were slaves in Egypt, *built for Pharaoh treasure cities, Pithom and Raamses.* When excavations were made in some mounds about thirty-five miles north of Cairo, the site of Pithom was determined.

Amelia Edwards, the well-known authority on Egypt, says, "It is a curious and interesting fact that the Pithom bricks are of three qualities. In the lower courses of these massive walls they are mixed with chopped straw; higher up when the straw may be supposed to have run short, the clay is found to be mixed with reeds . . . Finally when the reeds were used up, the bricks of the upper courses consist of mere Nile mud, with no building substance whatever." See what Exodus 5:6-19 says about this.

Pharaoh's plan was a very clever one. There was only one thing wrong with it—he left God out of his calculations. This is the trouble with the world today. Politicians and socialistic leaders and rulers have not found out whether their plans are in accord with God's plans. Consult God first in everything!

He that sitteth in the heavens shall laugh (Psalm 2:4). God must laugh often as He sees puny men and petty rulers defying Him and trying to thwart His plans. It is as if a number of ants built their hills on the tracks of a streamlined train and called a conference of ants to decide that the company had no authority to build on that right of way. While they were meeting, the great engine whizzed by and sent them all to their death.

There is joy and peace in the thought that we are in God's plan and under His protection.

THE EXODUS (Exodus 3; 4)

When the children of Israel were ready to become a nation, God raised up Moses to be their leader. He belonged to the tribe of Levi. (Levi was Jacob's third son. See Genesis 49.)

Baby Moses' life was in danger, for Pharaoh had directed that all Hebrew baby boys should be put to death. (Exodus 1:15-22) Here again we see Satan trying to thwart God's plan but again he was foiled. God used Pharaoh's daughter to make the future deliverer of Israel her son. (Exodus 2:10)

It is interesting to see how God works. There is delightful irony in the fact that after all of Pharaoh's planning to subjugate the children of Israel, the person who was to frustrate them all was not only brought up in Pharaoh's court, but Pharaoh paid all the bills for his education. How wonderfully God works. How weak man is when he puts his will up against God's.

It was when Moses was taking care of his sheep, just going about his daily task, that God came to call him. God always calls a man who is in his path of duty. God set a common little thorn bush ablaze and spoke to Moses from it. (Exodus 3)

Also notice that He called Moses by his name. God is very definite when He calls a person. He has a different task for each one of us. He says, "Saul, Peter, Moses," and then tells each one what He wants him to do. Each one of us has a God-given task. Let us never be sidetracked from it.

The desert did for Moses what Pharaoh's court could not do. It taught him what every child of God must learn—complete trust in the heavenly Father.

THE GREAT HERO MOSES

Moses' life may be divided into three periods of forty years each.

1. Forty years of education in Egypt as the son of Pharaoh's daughter. (Exodus 2:1-10; Acts 7:22,23.)

2. Forty years an exile in the desert of Arabia.

3. Forty years as leader of Israel.

Never did God give a man a harder task than He gave to Moses. God told Moses to lead a people out from the worst slavery that the world had ever known and make those slaves into a great nation. (Exodus 3) Slavery degrades a man. Freedom ennobles him. Only when man comes to the end of his resources can God do anything for him. "Man's extremity is God's opportunity." Therefore the children of Israel had to come to the end of their own strength in Egypt before they were willing to obey God. (Exodus 3:7)

The Book of Exodus teaches us that God will carry out His plan. Man may fail and Satan may attack, yet God has His plan.

For more than a thousand years before the days of Moses the literary art had been an important one in Egypt. They had recorded everything of importance on stone, leather and papyrus. Papyrus was used as early as 2700 B.C. Records on stone were more durable and every Pharaoh had carved on his palace walls and monuments the history of his reign.

Could you imagine that Moses was so stupid as to trust all the records of the children of Israel to oral traditions rather than writing?

We have only to look at the pyramids, the tombs of the Pharaohs, to have some idea of the civilization that existed between 4000 to 2000 B.C. The great Pyramid of Cheops covers thirteen acres. It contains thousands of stones with an average thickness of three feet and an average weight of two and a half tons. The Encyclopedia Brittanica says, "The brain power to which it testifies is as great as that of any modern man."

Stones were taken from a quarry twelve miles away and floated across the Nile. Then they were drawn up long, sloping construction ramps of soft earth by endless gangs of men, pulling at ropes to bring the huge blocks into place. It is said to have required 100,000 men ten years to build the causeway, and 360,000 men twenty years more to build the Pyramid itself. About 7,000,000 men from the working classes and slaves of Egypt were employed in forced labor.

This wonderful monument still stands, just outside the city of Cairo.

When Moses was prepared for his mission, God spoke from the burning bush near Sinai and called him to be the deliverer of Israel. He sent him back to Egypt. (Exodus 3; 4) The ten plagues, culminating in the death of the firstborn in Egyptian homes, made Pharaoh willing to permit the Israelites to leave the land. (Exodus 7–12)

Pharaoh's plans were overthrown, all his kingly commands came to naught, because One greater than Pharaoh willed it otherwise. This is true of every ruler who sets himself against God.

THE PASSOVER (Exodus 12–19)

This is indeed a sad scene. We hear the Egyptians wailing. Pharaoh had refused to let God's people go. His heart had become hardened. God had sent one plague after another until this dreadful night when God sent the tenth plague. The angel of the Lord destroyed the firstborn of man and beast among the houses of the Egyptians. The blood of a slain lamb put over the doorways of the homes of the children of Israel was a sign for the death angel to pass over and leave those homes untouched. (Ex. 12:3-13)

To commemorate this wonderful deliverance, God told the children of Israel to celebrate always the feast of the Passover. You remember Christ went to Jerusalem to this feast when He was a boy of twelve and we read of His return to Jerusalem at this time on several occasions. The Jews keep this feast today.

The passover lamb is the most perfect picture of Christ, our Redeemer, in the Old Testament. The blood of the passover lamb must not only be *shed* but it must be applied over the door. Not blood in the basin, but blood applied, saves a soul. Not all the blood shed on Calvary's cross can save a soul from death unless it is applied, then—*When I see the blood, I will pass over you* (Ex. 12:13).

It was not enough that Christ, our Passover (I Cor. 5:7) shed His blood on the cross. That was God's part. We must apply the blood to our hearts. (Titus 3:5) We must receive our Lord and Saviour into our hearts. (John 1:12) This is man's part.

The children of Israel, who had been slaves for the past four hundred years in Egypt, now leave with children, flocks, herds, loaded with the wealth and jewels of the Egyptians—the back pay which had been withheld from them during years of slavery.

Any Israelite who refused to go out when God had opened the way, never got another chance. It was the night of the Passover or never.

THE GIVING OF THE LAW (Exodus 20–24)

Now we see the children of Israel (about 3,000,000 in number) gathered in the wilderness at Mount Sinai to worship Jehovah God and to receive the Law which He would give them.

Up to this time all had been grace. God saw their need and heard their cry and had come down to deliver them. (Exodus 3:7-9) God had sent a leader; God had defeated their enemies; God had guided and fed them as they wandered through the wilderness.

Now God had brought them to Sinai. He gives the people a simple declaration of what He demands. (Exodus 20:1-17) The Law demands nothing short of perfection; but only one Man since it was given has ever kept it perfectly and He was the Lord from heaven. One hole in a bowl makes it useless to hold water. One flaw in keeping the Law mars the perfection God requires by the Law. (James 2:10)

Why was the Law given if no one could keep it? Galatians 3:24,25; 4:4,5; Romans 8:1-4 tell us why. That we might know how sinful we are. That we might see how weak we are. The Law is God's mirror to show us ourselves in God's eyes. The Law cannot cleanse us from sin, but it can show us our need. A mirror will show us that our face is soiled but the mirror cannot wash us clean.

When the Law shows us our weakness and sin, then God reveals the way to be cleansed. Read I John 1:9; Isaiah 1:16-18; Rev. 7:13-14.

THE BUILDING OF THE TABERNACLE (Exodus 25–40)

When the Holy Spirit spends much time on any one subject in the Word, we may be sure it is of tremendous importance and in some way tells us of Christ, for He is the theme of the Word.

We find over one third of the Book of Exodus (16 chapters) devoted to the details of the tabernacle.

On Mount Sinai, God gave Moses plans for a tabernacle which was to be the meeting place between God and the children of Israel for four hundred years until Solomon's temple should be built. It was a movable building, made of boards plated with gold. It was about 45 feet by 15 feet and was surrounded by a court 150 feet by 75 feet wide. (Ex. 27)

When man broke the Law, God revealed His plan whereby their sins could be dealt with and whereby they once again could worship Him.

The tabernacle was a perfect type of Christ. Christ is the only meeting place between a holy God and a lost sinner. (John 14:6) Some part of Christ's sacrifice was portrayed in the colors, designs, materials, sacrifices, and articles of furniture used in the tabernacle.

In the outer court we see the "brazen altar" on which the burnt offerings were sacrificed. Remember, Christ is our sin offering. (Exodus 27:1-8)

The "laver" was there for the cleansing of the priests before they could enter into the holy place to render their service. (Exodus 30:18)

In the holy place was the "golden candlestick" (Exodus 25:31-40), typifying Christ, the Light of the world, and the "table of shewbread" (Exodus 25:23-30), for Christ is the Bread of life, and the "golden altar of incense" (Exodus 30:1-10), symbolizing Christ's intercession for us.

Now if we draw back the beautiful veil (which typifies the body of Christ), we will see the "ark of the covenant," the symbol of God's presence. Into this "holy of holies" the high priest came only once a year to sprinkle the "blood of atonement." The Book of Hebrews tells us that Christ is not only our High Priest but that He was our atonement and so we can go into the holy of holies (the presence of God) at any time with boldness. The tabernacle, with the cloud of glory over it, taught the people that God was dwelling in their midst. (Exodus 25:8)

The contents of the tomb of Tutankamen, exhibited today in the museum at Cairo, give us some idea of what the "treasures in Egypt" (Heb. 11:24-26) were like in the days of Moses, although Moses lived about a century and a half before this Pharoah ascended the throne. A corridor filled with gold sarcophagi, chairs and lounges, shaving equipment, gauntlet gloves, bracelets and necklaces of beautiful workmanship tells us something of the grandeur of the day.

Come out for God! "Out of Egypt have I called my son." Come out, and keep coming out. This is the lesson of Exodus. (Remember, Egypt is the type of the world.)

THINK AND DO

The most important thing in the world today is Christian leadership. What qualities of leadership did Moses have that leaders today need? List them.

Do we find oppression and veritable slavery in portions of our world today? Discuss social injustice, minority groups (the American Negro, the Jew, etc.), crime, alcohol, the underprivileged.

How can we train for leadership in this world? in politics? in business? in social life?

Does the church call for leadership? What are its needs? Write to your denominational board and find what fields of service are open for youth.

INFORMATION PLEASE

1. Why was the name Exodus given to this book we are studying?
2. What instance do we find of God making His enemy pay for the education of one whom He is going to use for Himself? (Exodus 2:1-10)
3. When in history did the people bring such large offerings that the minister had to tell them to stop? (Exodus 36:1-7)
4. Tell of an instance when some men went to visit their brother and stayed so long they wore out their welcome?
5. How long was their visit? (Exodus 12:40,41)

Minimum Daily Requirements / Spiritual Vitamins

Sunday: BONDAGE Exodus 1:1-22

Monday: THE CALL OF MOSES Exodus 3–4

Tuesday: THE PLAGUES Exodus 7:20–11:10

Wednesday: THE PASSOVER Exodus 12:1-51

Thursday: THE LAW Exodus 20:1-26

Friday: THE WORSHIP Exodus 25:1-9; 28:1-14,30-43

Saturday: MOSES' COMMISSION RENEWED Exodus 33:12–34:17

Chapter 4

LET'S LOOK AT LEVITICUS

LEVITICUS PORTRAYS JESUS CHRIST,
OUR SACRIFICE FOR SIN

Some people do not see any profit in studying the
Book of Leviticus today. They say it is for the Jew.
Why do we, as Christians, need to study about the
sacrificing of bulls and goats? But remember this, each
offering points forward to Jesus Christ, our sacrifice for
sin. We see Him in every one. Think of this as you
study the book.

Notice how majestically Leviticus opens! *And the
Lord called.* Only two other books have a like beginning, Numbers and Joshua.

The fundamentals of true religion are set forth in Leviticus. The doctrine of the atonement for sin has first and foremost place as it has in all Scripture. The tabernacle, the altar, the priests, and the sacrifices are not needed any more, for Christ, our High Priest, has made them no longer necessary. The old Jewish priests were obliged to offer many sacrifices because these sacrifices were only symbolic of the blood of Christ which was to be shed to wash away sin. The blood of bulls and goats was not sufficient to take away sin. But Christ by His one offering hath perfected forever those who have accepted it. (Hebrews 10:14; 7:27)

Leviticus throws a flood of light on the question of capital and labor, land holding, marriage and divorce, and social questions and evils.

KEY THOUGHT

"Holiness unto the Lord" is the prominent thought in the entire Book of Leviticus. Everything in the book; priests, people, tabernacle with all its equipment, is holy and set apart for God. "Be ye holy as I am holy." (See Leviticus 11:44,45; 19:2; 20:7,26.)

This book insists upon holiness of the body as well as the soul. Leviticus teaches that the redeemed must be holy because their Redeemer is holy. (Rom. 12:1)

If the laws in the Book of Leviticus seem harsh and the penalties too severe, it is because they exhibit God's intolerance toward sin. It is because God is absolutely holy. This book not only shows that God is holy but that He is kind toward those that love Him. God shows us that "the shedding of blood" is necessary for "the remission of sin." God not only demanded holiness but He supplied it in His precious Son. (John 3:16)

In Exodus we see God giving Moses instructions for building the tabernacle.

In Leviticus there are instructions for worshiping in the tabernacle.

PURPOSE OF THE BOOK

This book was written for redeemed Israel. The Lord is giving His people instructions concerning various sacrifices and offerings He is showing them that the way to walk with God is by sacrifice and by separation.

He wanted His chosen people to live a life of holiness in fellowship with Himself. You know that before sin entered this world Adam and Eve had real fellowship with God. After they sinned, they hid themselves from their Maker. They feared God at that minute. They did not want to see Him. This is true of all sinners before they find Christ.

A people had been brought out of bondage and organized into a great nation. God had placed the tabernacle, a structure which signified His presence, in the very center of their life.

The Book of Exodus teaches the supreme purpose of worship in the life of the people, and the Book of Exodus tells how this worship should be carried on. The great question throughout the Book of Leviticus is, "How can an unholy people approach a holy God?"

THE PURPOSE OF THE OFFERINGS

God wants us to understand the awful reality of sin. *For all have sinned, and come short of the glory of God* (Romans 3:23). We must have the consciousness of sin before we can sense the need of a Saviour. One has to be sick before he feels the need of a doctor. God wanted the children of Israel to keep the consciousness of sin before them by daily offering a sacrifice.

Sin is anything in your life that displeases God. Anything!

A father in anger struck his child and hit him against a hot stove. The child was horribly burned. At first they despaired of his life, but after days of anxiety he recovered. The wounds were deep. Every time that father looked upon the scarred face of his son, he was conscious of his sin.

God knew that as often as man looked upon the bleeding sacrifice, he would be conscious of his sin and realize that the "wages of sin is death." That bleeding animal reminded man that death was sin's penalty.

One day the Lamb of God was going to shed His blood for the sins of the world.

Sin may be forgiven, but it must be punished. God could not forgive sin unless His Son had borne the penalty for the sins of the world upon the cross. (John 3:16) *He was wounded for our transgressions, He was bruised for our iniquities* (Isaiah 53:5).

The cross of Christ stands as God's estimate of what sin really is, and how much it costs. Sin is the most expensive thing in the universe. We have the cure for sin. It always works! It has washed millions and millions of souls. It is the only cure in the world.

Christ can save to the uttermost—anytime, anywhere. God has furnished the way for everyone.

In these offerings we will see soul-stirring views of the person and work of our blessed Lord and Saviour, Jesus Christ. There are five kinds of offerings described. It needs a great variety of types to portray the perfect completeness of Christ's sacrifice.

THE FIVE OFFERINGS
THE BURNT OFFERING (Leviticus 1)

Here we have a type of Christ offering Himself without spot to God. We see Christ on the cross doing the will of God. His last prayer was *not my will, but thine, be done* (Luke 22:42).

The burnt offering could be a bullock, a ram, turtle dove or pigeon. There is a beautiful thought in the variety of the material which was permitted. The poor

33

man's pair of pigeons burned with an odor as sweet as the rich man's bull.

The worshiper led the animal, possibly resisting, by some rude halter to the tabernacle. There, by the altar, he stood with his hand on the head of his offering, indicating that it was his offering. He then killed the victim with one swift cut. The attending priest caught the warm blood in a basin and sprinkled it upon the altar. Then the offerer skinned the animal and cut up the sacrifice. His part was done. He stood by with bloody hands to watch the priest.

Soon the odor of the burning flesh and the smoke filled the air. What a sight it must have been when on great occasions hundreds of burnt offerings were made in succession!

This offering signified the dedication of the offerer. Why was the burnt offering first? Because sacrifice comes first. No one begins with God until he has yielded himself to God, and yielded all. The lamb without blemish (Lev. 1:3) consumed by the fire showed that the dedication must be perfect in quality as well as in quantity.

"Take my life and let it be consecrated, Lord, to Thee."

MEAL OFFERING (Leviticus 2)

As the burnt offering typifies Christ in death, so the meal offering typifies Him in life. There is no blood-shedding in this offering, just a beautiful type of Christ as He lived and walked on earth. Every true Christian should know the pure, perfect life of our blessed Lord. The subject of the person of Christ is an important one. There is nothing the heart desires that it cannot find in Christ.

The materials used were flour (fine meal), oil (type of the Holy Spirit), salt (His words were seasoned with salt), and frankincense (that when the sacrifice was put on the fire the sweet odor might ascend to the Father).

The meal offering represents the daily devotion of the believer. There must be an offering of a perfect service as well as a perfect life. This represents our very best, the gift of a life.

PEACE OFFERING (Leviticus 3)

No one offering furnishes a complete picture of Christ. All must be put together. The peace offering should be ot the herd of the flock but it must be without blemish, as all the sacrifices. Again the hand of the offerer is placed on the victim. (Lev. 3:8) Part of the offering was burned by fire and part eaten by the worshiper. It is the symbol of communion. Remember, Christ is our peace and our exceeding joy. There is One who has made peace for us and is our Peace. Because of Christ's perfection, we can sit at the table with the Father, not in our own filthy rags or in any robe that we have made, but in the best robe of Christ's righteousness. If sin be in question, communion is out of question.

SIN OFFERING (Leviticus 4:1–35; 5:1–13)

In this offering we see an acknowledgment of sin. *If a soul shall sin . . . let him bring* (Lev. 4:2,3). This offering is for expiation. In the other offerings the offerer comes as a worshiper, but here as a convicted sinner. God holds us accountable for our sin. We are like criminals who have been tried, found guilty, and sentenced to death.

TRESPASS OFFERING (Leviticus 5:14–6:7)

This offering was provided for definite acts of wrong doing—first, against God, and second, against man. (Lev. 5:15) If a positive wrong were done, even in ignorance, it could not be overlooked.

God can forgive any trespass, but He can overlook none. God made a covenant with His Son to deliver men, not because men deserved such mercy, or because they could demand it, but simply because it was His good pleasure to do it. (Titus 3:4-6)

It is a grave mistake to suppose that a man is safe and right if he lives up to the dictates of his own conscience. God has scales. God looks at the heart and the motive as well as the deed. Our conscience must always be turned to God's will if it is to be accurate.

If a man's conscience is set right, his conduct must be righteous. *Whosoever doeth not righteousness is not of God* (I John 3:10). Man must be just as orthodox in his conduct as he is in his creed.

The precious blood of Christ has settled all sin questions, whether it be a sin toward God or man. The cross has divinely met all. No one was ever regenerated except at the cross. When the divine right was infringed upon, only blood atoned. *Without shedding of blood is no remission* (Hebrews 9:22). In our relation to others restitution must be made, wrongs must be righted. (Matthew 5:23-24) But mere restitution will not do. There must be shedding of blood, for "the wages of sin is death." The blood is the life. The life of Christ is the blood of Christ. Christ's blood cleanses from all sin. When God says "cleanses," He means He really cleans from all sin.

Sin against a neighbor is looked upon as sin against God. A practical lesson for us here is that we must make restitution for the wrong which we have done as far as it is in our power. Remember to right wrongs in your life. Often it is hard to admit your wrong to the person you have sinned against. It often costs to do it.

His grace is perfect, therefore He can forgive all.
His holiness is perfect, therefore He can pass over nothing.

THE PRIEST (Leviticus 8–10)

We have been studying the great subject of sacrifice. Now we approach the great subject of priesthood. These two subjects are closely connected.

The sinner needs a sacrifice.
The believer needs a priest.

Christ is both to us! He was our spotless Sacrifice, and now He is our great High Priest. (Hebrews 7:27) A priest is one who offers sacrifices. He is also one who intercedes and one who is a go-between, or mediator, between God and man. (Hebrews 2:17)

Although we are fully delivered from the penalty of sin and accepted in Christ, nevertheless we are weak and very apt to wander and fall. Therefore we need the ceaseless ministry of our great High Priest. *He ever liveth to make intercession for them* (Hebrews 7:25). We must be freed from the power of sin for *sin shall not have dominion over you* (Romans 6:14). Some day we shall be freed from the presence of sin. We shall be made like Christ for we shall see Him as He is.

In Leviticus 8, we read of the consecration of Aaron, the high priest, and his sons. In the midst of a solemn assembly the priests were cleansed and Aaron was arrayed in the garments of his sacred office. Then followed the holy rites of consecration. The ceremony was repeated daily for seven days. Then their priestly work began. The first act of Aaron, the high priest, was that of presenting the sin offering and the burnt offering for himself. Then the sin, burnt, and peace offerings were made for the people. Aaron blessed the people and the glory of the Lord was shown and supernatural fire consumed the sacrifice.

THE EIGHT FEASTS

As the first part of the Book of Leviticus has to do with offerings and the offerers, so the last part of the book deals with feasts and feasters.

The calendar of feasts is given in Leviticus 16, and 23–25. Every religion has its feasts and festivals. They are necessary to its existence. They keep alive its memories. We are prone to forget if we do not see. There is enthusiasm in numbers.

FEAST OF THE SABBATH (Leviticus 23:1-3)

The foremost place was given to the Sabbath. The Jews' worship of Jehovah was insured by the laws regarding the Sabbath. They were required to keep the day holy and distinct from other days. It was designed to turn their thoughts to God and make them think of Him.

The Christian celebrates the first day of the week instead of the seventh because he worships a living Christ who rose from the grave on the first day of the week.

FEAST OF THE PASSOVER (Leviticus 23:4,5)

The Passover spoke of redemption and was celebrated every spring at our Easter time. It was the Fourth of July for the children of Israel. They did not celebrate it by fireworks and parades but by a great service of worship to God. Every Jew who could, made his way to Jerusalem. (Jesus went as a boy. Luke 2:41-52)

This feast celebrates the redemption of Israel from Egyptian bondage. The Jews celebrate events, not men. The Lord's Supper is a memorial of our redemption as the Passover is a memorial of Israel's redemption.

Purge out therefore the old leaven, that ye may be a new lump, as ye are unleavened. For even Christ our passover is sacrificed for us (I Cor. 5:7).

FEAST OF PENTECOST (Leviticus 23:15-22)

This feast was observed fifty days after the feast of the first fruits. This feast of the first fruits typifies

Christ's resurrection and ours. (I Cor. 15:20) It was fifty days after Christ's resurrection that the Holy Spirit descended upon the disciples, and the Church was born. Pentecost was the birthday of the Church. The death and resurrection of Christ had to be accomplished before the descent of the Holy Spirit.

THE FEAST OF THE TRUMPETS (Leviticus 23:23-25)

This was the New Year's day of the children of Israel. It was celebrated in the fall around October. This feast points forward to the future gathering of the dispersed people of Israel. (Zech. 14)

THE DAY OF ATONEMENT (Leviticus 23:26-32)

This was the greatest day in the history of God's chosen people. On this day the sins of the nation were confessed. Confession is always the first step toward righteousness. It reveals a right attitude toward sin. It leads to a desire for forgiveness. God says, *If we confess our sins, He is faithful and just to forgive us our sins, and to cleanse us from all unrighteousness* (I John 1:9).

This was the only day in the year when the high priest was permitted to enter the holy of holies. He went in with an offering for the atonement of the sin of the people. Atonement means "cover." This offering "covered' the sins of the people until the great sacrifice on Calvary was made. None of these offerings "took away" those sins.

THE FEAST OF TABERNACLES (Leviticus 23:33-36)

This was the last feast of the year. It commemorated the time when the children of Israel lived in tents during their wilderness journey. It was celebrated in the fall of the year and lasted a week. The people lived in booths out-of doors and heard the law read.

The Feast of the Passover and the Feast of Tabernacles kept before the children of Israel the marvelous way in which they were delivered from Egypt and were sustained in the wilderness. God did not want them to forget the way in which the gods of Egypt were utterly discredited and the great nation of Egypt humbled.

THE SABBATIC YEAR (Leviticus 25)

This was the year of meditation and devotion. It was a year-long Sabbath. The purpose and character of the Sabbath was magnified. God impressed it upon the minds of the people, keeping them from any kind of labor for the extent of a year. This he did every seven years.

God wanted to impress upon them that the very land was holy unto Him. This is why Palestine is called the Holy Land. There was a quiet over the whole land during these days. All breathed the spirit of rest and meditation. All industry ceased. Every day was like the Sabbath, and the minds of the people were kept on the things of the Lord. The law was read. There were no debts to worry or mar the spirit of the people during this holy year. This time exerted a great influence upon the lives of the people.

THE YEAR OF JUBILEE (Leviticus 25:8–24)

This was celebrated every fiftieth year. (Lev. 25:10) Every slave was freed, all land was returned to its rightful owner, all debts were cancelled. Everyone had a new start. This gave no opportunity for large syndicates of ownership.

THINK AND DO

Why should a Christian study the Book of Leviticus?

Why is God so intolerant toward sin?

When you look at the cross of Calvary, what do you think God's estimate of sin really is?

Why did Christ have to offer His life as a sacrifice for sin?

How does Leviticus prove the statement found in Hebrews 9:22, *without shedding of blood is no remission* of sin?

Who is our High Priest?

Peter says we are all *kings and priests*. What does he mean? (See also I Peter 2:5.)

Is it possible for men to break God's laws? Illustrate how God's law breaks men. If man could break God's laws, the universe would fly to pieces.

What Old Testament law is found in Numbers 32:23? How does Paul state it in Romans 6:23?

Minimum Daily Requirements / Spiritual Vitamins

Sunday: BURNT OFFERING Leviticus 1
Monday: THE PRIESTS Leviticus 8
Tuesday: PURE FOOD LAWS Leviticus 11
Wednesday: THE DAY OF ATONEMENT Leviticus 16
Thursday: THE FEASTS OF JEHOVAH Leviticus 23
Friday: GOD'S PLEDGE Leviticus 26
Saturday: DEDICATION Leviticus 27

41

Chapter 5

LET'S LOOK AT NUMBERS

*NUMBERS PORTRAYS JESUS CHRIST,
OUR "LIFTED-UP ONE"*

The children of Israel were saved to serve. So is every child of God today.

WARNING!

Beware of unbelief! The apostle Paul says to us, *Ye did run well; who did hinder you* (Galatians 5:7)? Unbelief hinders blessing. God tells why we cannot enter into His blessings. (Heb. 3:19)

This book might be called "Wilderness Wanderings." It extends from Sinai to the border of Canaan, the land of promise, and covers a period of forty years.

Numbers is also called the Book of the March and the Roll Call. (Numbers 33:1,2)

It might, too, be called the Book of Murmurings, because from beginning to end it is filled with the spirit of rebellion against God. Read what God says about this in Psalm 95:10.

The key thought is discipline. Numbers is the fourth book of Moses. Someone has said that the order of the books is as follows:

1. In Genesis we see man ruined.
2. In Exodus, man redeemed.
3. In Leviticus, man worshiping.
4. In Numbers, man serving.

This is the order the Lord lays down. Only a saved man can serve and worship God. Remember, we are saved to serve.

PERSONNEL OF THE BOOK

If you know the following five names, you will master the story of the Book of Numbers.

Moses, the great leader.

Aaron, the high priest, Moses' brother.

Miriam, Moses' and Aaron's sister.

Joshua and *Caleb,* the two spies who dared to believe God, the only men of their generation who lived to enter Canaan.

PREPARATION FOR THE JOURNEY (Numbers 1–12)

As the book opens we see the children of Israel in the wilderness of Sinai. The Law had been given, the tabernacle had been built, and the priests had been assigned to their service. Now God was going to prepare the nation for its work. The teachings of this book are very applicable to the Christian life in this present evil world.

Order is heaven's first law. We see God numbering and arranging the tribes (chapters 1 and 2), choosing and assigning duties to the priests and Levites (chapters 3 and 4). God is the author of order.

The thought of God numbering His people and gathering them about Himself is most precious to our hearts. He dwelt in the camp. The twelve tribes guarded the tabernacle of the Lord. The Levites encamped directly around the court, and Moses and Aaron and the priests guarded the entrance whereby God was approached.

The circumference of the entire camp is supposed to have been about twelve miles. What an imposing sight the camp must have been to the outward eyes, in the midst of the desert, with God stretching over them in a cloud by day and fire by night. (Numbers 9:15-23) He was their night lamp and their day shade. Their shoes did not wear out nor their garments wax old. Think of 600,000 men twenty years old and upward, and about 3,000,000 men, women and children in all this great camp! But the most glorious thing was that God was in the midst.

Here were about 3,000,000 people on a sterile desert, not a blade of grass, not a drop of water, no visible means of support. How were they to be fed? God was there! How were they to trace their way through a howling wilderness where there was no path? God was there!

God's presence provides everything! What? Are these 3,000,000 to be fed on air? Who has charge of the commissary? Where is the baggage? Who is to attend to the clothing? God was there! In faith's arithmetic God is the only figure that counts. (Jesus fed 5,000 with five loaves and two small fishes.)

No one had gone before to blaze a trail for the children of Israel. There was not a footprint, not a landmark. It is much like our life as a Christian today. We are passing through a trackless desert—a moral wilderness. There is no trail. We would not know where to walk except for one little sentence from the lips of the Lord, *I am the way* (John 14:6). He will guide us step by step. There is no uncertainty, for He said, *He that followeth me shall not walk in darkness* (John 8:12).

In the first chapter, Moses is commanded to take a census. The Lord knows all by name that are His. (II Tim. 2:19; Phil. 4:3) Even the hairs of our head are numbered. Each individual is important to God. How wonderful to know that He cares for each of His children.

For Christians, too, there is a census, for Christ numbers His jewels and *knoweth them that are His. A book of remembrance was written before him.* (Read Mal. 3:16,17.)

In this chapter we find the declaration of their pedigree. Can you trace your genealogy to the risen Lord? Are you sure of your pedigree? (John 1:12)

Sin crept into this well-ordered camp life. The people began to murmur against God. God sent judgment of fire. (Numbers 11:1-3) Then they complained about their food. (11:4) It seemed monotonous. They longed for the garlic and onions of Egypt, and they wanted fish. As a result of their complaining, God sent them quails for thirty days. They made gluttons of themselves *and while the flesh was yet between their teeth, ere it was chewed, the wrath of the Lord was kindled against the people, and the Lord smote the people with a very great plague* (Numbers 11:33). Many became ill and died.

Then we read of the sin of Aaron, the high priest, and Miriam, the sister of Moses. God had chosen Moses to be the leader of this great people and Aaron and Miriam were only his assistants. Jealousy crept into their hearts. They wanted more honor. Read of Miriam's terrible punishment. She was smitten with leprosy for seven days. (Numbers 12:1-16)

We find the invitation of God's marching host to the people round about them, *Come thou with us, and we will do thee good: for the Lord hath spoken good concerning Israel* (Numbers 10:29). Do we say this to those about us?

WILDERNESS WANDERINGS (Numbers 13–20)

Think of the lost years from Kadesh back to Kadesh because men would not believe God. After two years in the wilderness, the children of Israel could have gone into the land of promise immediately had it not been for the sin of unbelief. They listened to the discouraging words of the spies.

When the spies came back and told them about the giants in the land and the high and fenced cities, their hearts failed them. They would not listen to Joshua and Caleb who agreed to all that was told, but added, *Let us go up at once, and possess it; for we are well able to overcome it* (Numbers 13:30). But the people would not trust God. They said, *Let us make a captain, and let us return into Egypt* (Numbers 14:4).

When they refused to enter Canaan, the door was closed to them. It meant wandering in the wilderness for forty years. God said that He would not allow any of those who were over twenty years old to enter Canaan, except Joshua and Caleb.

Eleven days from the land of promise! But they turned back. They could have made eleven days of progress, but they chose forty years of wandering.

One of the reports of the spies was that there were giants in the land and that the Israelites were as grasshoppers in their sight. (Numbers 13:33)

This record tells the story of many a Christian life and in part the story of every life. Giants of selfishness and greed, far outranking the Anakims, oppose our advance! But when the returns are all in, the fact remains that there is One with us stronger than they!

Like the ten, we can be pessimists; or like the two, optimists. Like the ten, we can put difficulties between us and God and say we are not able, or like the two, we can put God between the difficulties and ourselves and say we are able!

We start out with high hope in the enthusiasm of our first love. Yonder lies the land of possibilities and achievement. Then the giants appear—giants of opposition from without; giants of fear from within. Our faith fails. We forget God. We compare our difficulties with our own strength rather than committing them to the great arm of God. Then we turn back into the wilderness of half trust, half victory and whole despair.

Numbers 33 is the pitiful log book of this journey, *And they departed from Hazeroth, and pitched in Rithmah. And they departed from Rithmah, and pitched at Rimmon-parez. And they departed from Rimmon-parez, and pitched in Libnah* etc., to the end of this dismal chapter! Going, going, pitching, and departing, but never arriving anywhere. An endless circle of aimless wandering with no success. When we doubt God we find this to be our experience, too. We feel defeated and discouraged. We wander around but never accomplish anything. It is like a swinging door— lots of motion but getting no place.

Before this scene ends we find Israel murmuring again, this time because of the shortage of water. They complained bitterly to Moses and Aaron and said they wished they had never been brought out of Egypt. The land was dry and parched and there was no water to drink. Moses and Aaron again went to God. He told

Moses to take his rod and speak to the rock before the people, and the rock would give forth water.

Moses' patience was at an end. The people had complained about everything. In a fit of rage he called the people rebels and instead of speaking to the rock he struck it. The water gushed out. Even though Moses disobeyed, God was faithful and kept His promise. That stream may still be flowing, even today. The Turkish army put in a pipeline and got their water from this district during World War I. Kadesh-barnea is a beautiful oasis. Ruins of the ancient city of Kadesh are to be found here today.

Is it not sad that even children of God fail under testing? Moses' error was great, yet it showed him to be merely a man like us. Moses put himself up as God—*Hear now, ye rebels; must we fetch you water out of this rock* (Numbers 20:10)? This dishonored Jehovah God. Because Moses smote the rock a second time (see first time, Exodus 17:5,6) instead of speaking to it, he was not permitted to enter the promised land. Christ, like the rock, was to be smitten once for our sins (I Cor. 10:4) He need not be smitten again.

There are three ways of knowing men, a rabbi in the Talmud says:

In their cups,

With their cash,

In their wrath.

How true it is that ill-behavior at the table discloses bad culture; ill-conduct in business reveals the unscrupulous; ill-speaking in wrath proclaims the ignoble.

ON TO CANAAN (Numbers 21–36)

As this scene opens we discover that all the Israelites who left Egypt had died except Moses, Aaron, Joshua, Caleb, Miriam, and the children who were under twenty years of age when the spies entered the land. Why was this?

One day while they were yet in Kadesh, Miriam, Moses' sister, and Aaron, his brother, now over 100 years old, died.

Israel was to move on again. They started from Kadesh-barnea, this time with faces set resolutely toward the land of promise. The way was difficult, much harder than before, but faith had been renewed, discipline had done its work, and the arm of God went forth conquering and to conquer.

Learn here the lesson of God's second best. He offers the perfect way and we refuse it. It is gone forever. Every male over twenty years of age who refused to go into the land of promise the first time died in the wilderness. Not one entered the land except Joshua and Caleb.

But God was kind, and He sets before us another way, a second best; it may even be a third, for His mercy is wonderful. He forgives us seventy times seven. He brings us through, provides for us, never failing in His grace, but, oh, how much we miss and how many burdens we have to bear by not taking the first and the best. How costly this is!

Israel was complaining again, although over and over again God had proven to them that His way is best. Discontent and murmuring seem to have been ingrained habits of the children of Israel. Grumbling is the easiest thing in the world to learn. "No talent, no self-denial, no brains, no character is required to set up the grumbling business," are the words written in a large office.

What's the use of grumbling? It never makes a heavy burden light. It never subtracts from ills. Instead it always adds to them.

They battled with the Canaanites and became discouraged. Then they grumbled because they had to march around the land of Edom instead of through it. They growled again against God and against Moses because they loathed the manna. (Numbers 21:5) They never were content.

This time God sent fiery serpents among the people, which caused suffering and death. After they confessed their sins, Moses prayed for the deliverance of his people. God did not take away the serpents but told Moses to make a brass serpent and fasten it to a pole so that all could see it. As soon as they looked, they would live. (See Numbers 21:6-9.)

The Bible reveals that the whole human family has felt the Serpent's sting of sin which means death. The only way man can live is by looking to the One who took upon Himself the likeness of men and was lifted up on the cross to take the sting of death upon Himself. If we look upon Him, our Saviour, we shall live. (John 3:14,15)

THINK AND DO

Tell the story of the Book of Numbers by following Moses, Aaron, Miriam, Joshua and Caleb.

What kept the children of Israel from entering the Land of Promise when they had reached its very door?

What is the greatest sin of men today that keeps them from accepting Christ as Saviour?

Why was Moses' sin so great? (Numbers 20:2-13)

What story in Numbers tells us of "life for a look"?

Is the voice of the majority always the voice of God? (The spies)

Do we as Americans ask for God's guidance in national affairs? Do we pray for leading as a nation? Do you think America is wandering in confusion and fear because they can no longer say "in God we trust"?

50

Minimum Daily Requirements / Spiritual Vitamins

Sunday: THE GUIDING CLOUD Numbers 9:15-23
Monday: THE REPORT OF THE SPIES Numbers 13:16-33
Tuesday: ISRAEL'S UNBELIEF Numbers 14:1-45
Wednesday: WATER FROM THE ROCK Numbers 20:1-13
Thursday: THE BRAZEN SERPENT Numbers 21:1-9
Friday: BALAAM'S ASS Numbers 22:1-41
Saturday: THE CITIES OF REFUGE Numbers 35:6-34

Chapter 6

LET'S LOOK AT DEUTERONOMY

*DEUTERONOMY PORTRAYS JESUS CHRIST,
OUR TRUE PROPHET*

STOP AND THINK—THEN GO ON AND DO

"Observe to do" is the word of Moses to the people. He wanted them to be *doers of the word, and not hearers only* (James 1:22).

This book shows the blessings of obedience and the curse of disobedience.

Everything depends on obedience—life itself, possession of the promised land, victory over foes, prosperity and happiness. We find this book teaching the inflexibility of the law. "Thou shalt" and "thou shalt not" occur over and over again—"a blessing if ye obey" and "a curse if ye will not obey."

The Book of Deuteronomy is a collection of the orations and songs of Moses which he gave as his farewell to the children of Israel.

Deuteronomy is a Book of Remembrance. The name Deuteronomy means "second law" which indicates that the law is repeated. This Moses did to remind the people what God had done for them and what they were to do to serve Him when they reached the promised land. It omits the things that relate to the priests and Levites and includes the things that the people should know.

This book is the last of the five books of Moses. You often hear these five books called the Pentateuch, simply meaning five books.

Deuteronomy covers only about two months, including the thirty days of mourning for Moses.

Moses was the writer but not the author of the Pentateuch. See chapter two. Over five hundred times in these first five books, we find expressions like "The Lord spake," "God said," etc. Who is the divine Author of the Bible? (II Peter 1:21)

The Christian heart always quickens its beat when it

THE PENTATEUCH SUMMARIZED

Genesis tells of the beginnings of the chosen nation Israel.

Exodus relates the organization of the people into a nation and the giving of the law.

Leviticus tells the way this people were to worship God.

Numbers gives a story of the wanderings of this people.

Deuteronomy relates the final preparation for entering the promised land.

comes to Deuteronomy, for this book was a favorite with our Saviour. From this book He quoted in His conflict with the adversary. These passages were His weapons with which He repelled the tempter: Matt. 4:1-11; Luke 4:1-13; and Deut. 8:3; 6:16; 6:13; and 10:20. Christ took Deuteronomy as His code of conduct. Thus this Book of Deuteronomy, God's book on obedience, Moses' last charge to his people, seems to have about it the peculiar blessing and protection of Christ Himself.

These discourses were not spoken to those who had been at Sinai. What happened at Sinai? (Exodus 19:20–20:18) These had all died in the wilderness. Why? (Numbers 14:23-34) Therefore every loyal Israelite pondered on them, yes, even learned them by heart. Can we do any better? Do you store God's Word away in your heart? What does the psalmist tell us will happen if we do? (Psalm 119:11)

If you want a taste of heaven on earth become familiar with Deuteronomy. Catch step with Moses and march ahead by way of the Honey-Land. (Canaan, a land flowing with milk and honey. Exodus 3:8)

"Brethren," a negro once said, "when I get to the gates of heaven, if they shut me out, I'll say, 'Anyhow, I had a good time gettin' here.'"

Are you having a good time on your way to heaven? God *hath blessed us with all spiritual blessings in heavenly places in Christ* but we must appropriate and possess them by faith. (Eph. 1:3)

MOSES' FIRST ADDRESS – "LOOKING BACK"
(Chapters 1–4)

As the book opens we see the children of Israel on the border of the land of Canaan, in a place where eleven days' journey, some forty years ago, could have brought them. Yet it had taken them forty years. How slowly they covered the ground! What windings and turnings! How often we have to go over the same ground again and again. We marvel at Israel's slowness. We can rather marvel at out own! We, like them, are kept back by unbelief. How ashamed we should be at the time it takes us to learn our lessons! God is such a faithful teacher. He never lets us pass on to another grade until we are ready.

How deplorable is unbelief! God never fails us when we put our trust in Him, but He cannot do many mighty works because of our unbelief. (Matthew 13:58)

Nearly five hundred years before, God had promised to Abraham and his seed this great and wondrous land upon whose borders they were standing. (Genesis 17:8) They were ready now to enter in after all the years of anticipation and hope. The closing chapters of Numbers found them camped by the Jordan, waiting to go over into the goodly land itself.

As we shall see, God is putting the conditions of their entering and holding the land before the children of Israel in Deuteronomy. We see all these conditions summed up in one word: Obedience.

In the first four books of the Pentateuch God is choosing Israel. Now He is letting Israel choose Him.

Only Caleb and Joshua were left from those who had come out of Egypt. All the others had died and a new generation had taken their place. These younger men had suffered hardships in the wilderness and were ready for conquest! But Moses must rehearse the Law to them. He knows his work is finished, for God has told him another will lead them into Canaan. (Numbers 20:12)

This grand old man was now one hundred and twenty years old. We see him giving his farewell address to the people whom he had led these past forty years. He stood erect and spoke with a clear tone, for it is said that *his eye was not dim, nor his natural force abated* (Deuteronomy 34:7).

Moses gives the children of Israel a look back. He recalls the history of Israel and reviews their wanderings. He reminds them of God's faithfulness and urges them to be grateful and obedient. He likens God's care of them to a loving father who cherishes his little ones, lest they should be lost in the wilderness, or be injured by the heat of the sun. He supplied all their needs; they lacked no good thing. (Deuteronomy 2:7)

He spoke to his beloved people in the most earnest and eloquent way and appealed to them to serve and obey God. His words still echo down the corridors of time and it is well for us to hear the words of this hero of the ages!

Moses' work was done. He had spent the last forty years of his life in delivering his people from the bondage of Egypt, in guiding them through the many dangers that confronted them. He trained them, gave them forms of government, laws, religious institutions and moulded them into a nation.

The children of Israel were now at the end of their journey, in the plain east of the Jordan, overlooking the land they had come so far to possess. It lay before them in the glories of the springtime. But the impassable Jordan river rolled between, and walled cities rose up in seemingly impregnable strength. The people were like young men leaving school or college to enter their life's work.

MOSES' SECOND ADDRESS — "LOOKING UP"
(Chapters 5–26)

In Deuteronomy 12:1 we see the key to this section. *These are the statutes and judgments, which ye shall observe to do in the land.* Israel was going into a new land and everything would depend on their constant and intelligent obedience to God who was giving them the land. God wanted to teach Israel the love which is the real fulfilling of the Law. (Romans 13:8-10; Matthew 22:37-40)

Moses now sets forth the Law simply and clearly so that it would take a living hold of the people. God says, "Ye are My people; I love you. I have chosen you; I am in the midst of you. I will protect you. I am only asking you to obey Me for your good." He says, "Be ye holy; for I am holy." Since God's people are His, He wants them to walk in the world in the ways that befit them, separating themselves from evil. (Chapter 14) They should show charity toward their fellows. (Chapter 15) They must gather together to worship. (Deut. 16; Hebrews 10:25)

Today, people are careless about church-going and worship. This speaks of spiritual decay. God demands discipline. (Deuteronomy 17)

In Deuteronomy 18, God tells us of the great Prophet, the Lord Jesus Christ. He alone knows the future. In this day, many are turning to enchanters, soothsayers, fortune-tellers, mediums, consulters with familiar spirits and the black art of sorcery of every description. Spiritualism is rampant today! If you want to know what God thinks about the modern seance look up Isaiah 8:19,20; Lev. 19:31; 20:6; and study the dark story in I Samuel 28 in the light of I Chron. 10:13.

God showed the Israelites that their highest duty was to exhibit the spirit of loving obedience. They were to be thankful, yes, really thankful. They were to be full of joy and gladness. Why shouldn't they be joyful in the best land on earth, and with such a God as Jehovah? Surely they ought to be glad and love their God with all their heart.

But Moses' heart was burdened because he knew that Israel had a hard heart and was self-willed. (Deut. 31:24-29)

How many children, in these days of ours (see their description by Paul in II Timothy 3:1-9), should die, under the solemn command of Deut. 21:18-21.

Note this! A child disobedient and rebellious toward his parents is an abomination in God's sight.

If we read Deuteronomy 21:22,23 and compare it with John 19:31, we see why Christ was accursed as He hung between heaven and earth on the cross. In Galatians 3:10-13 we read that He is cursed because He was bearing our sin. (II Cor. 5:21) What does Paul say? (II Cor. 5:14,15)

MOSES' THIRD ADDRESS — "LOOKING OUT"
(Chapters 27–33)

We see Moses giving the people some solemn warnings. He first spoke of the blessings that the children of Israel could enjoy if they would be obedient. He then told them the results of disobedience. Misfortune would follow them in everything they would undertake—in business, in farming, and in health. They would suffer for their disobedience to God. (Chapter 28:15 to end of chapter)

Deuteronomy 28 is a most remarkable chapter. It traces what Israel might have been through obedience (1-14) and is yet to be in the millennial age to come. (See Isaiah 60–62; Zech. 14:8-21; Jer. 31:1-9; Deut. 30:1-10; Rom. 11:25-31.)

Verses 47-49 tell of the Roman invasion, 70 A.D., under Titus. This was indeed a bloody page of history!

Verses 63-67 describe the Jew today. God spoke this more than 3000 years ago. Chapter 28 leaves Israel where that nation is today—"scattered."

1. "SCATTERED"—He shall be scattered from one end of the earth to the other.

Today the Jew is everywhere—there are German Jews, Russian Jews, Italian Jews, American Jews, etc.

2. "RESTLESS"—No rest for the Jew in these countries. (Verse 65)

3. "SORROWFUL"—The Jew today has a trembling heart and sorrow fills him. Think of the way he was treated before and during World War II. (Verses 65-67) God foretold all this to him!

Moses speaks to Joshua, his personal attendant, through the wilderness. He was one of the spies who dared to believe God. He was now 80 years old and Moses was committing to him the leadership of this great people! Read his words in Deuteronomy 31:7,8.

The charge that Moses gave to the people and to Joshua was built on one great fact, "The Lord is with you; be strong." If God is present, fear is baseless!

This grand old man, one hundred and twenty years of age, stood a witness to the grace of God. He sang a song for Israel. (Chapter 32) Moses had celebrated the deliverance of Israel from Egypt with a song (Exodus 15), and now he closes his life's work with another. He wrote a third which we know as the ninetieth Psalm. Christians have always had a song! And in heaven throughout the ages everyone will sing!

After the song and final words of blessing, Moses goes up to Nebo's heights and there God shows him the promised land toward which his face had so long been set. Moses died there and God buried His servant in the valley and was there to comfort him. "God buries the workman but carries on the work."

Whether Moses himself wrote Deuteronomy 34 by revelation or whether Joshua added it later is immaterial. Moses climbed Mt. Pisgah, saw the promised land

and never came back. We know he died there and the Lord buried him, no one knows where. Someone said, "God buried his burial."

The horde of slaves made into a nation by Moses wept for him thirty days. Had it not been for their perversity they might still have had him with them.

Why do you think Moses' grave was hidden? No doubt it would have become the object of superstitious idolatry. It is well, for this same reason, that Jesus' true grave is unknown.

We read of Moses again in the Gospels. One day Jesus took Peter, James and John and climbed up Mt. Hermon in the northern part of Palestine. Then Moses and Elijah appeared and talked with Jesus about His coming death. (Matthew 17:1-3)

THINK AND DO

Some nuggets for your red pencil: Deuteronomy 4:29,39; 5:29; 6:4,5,12; 8:3; 18:15; 20:4; 31:6-8; 32:10-12; 33:3,12,25-27; 34:10.

What does God say about fortune-tellers?

Thousands travel to Mecca to the tomb of Mohammed. Why is it that men never make a pilgrimage to Moses' tomb?

Would you like to know how a national hero feels when denied the privilege of setting forth on his dreamed of Shangri-la? If so, read Deuteronomy. Read Moses' song in chapter 32.

Minimum Daily Requirements / Spiritual Vitamins

Sunday: FORWARD MARCH Deut. 1:6-46
Monday: INSTRUCTIONS Deut. 5:1-33; 6:4-18
Tuesday: THE MESSIAH, PROPHET Deut. 18:15-22
Wednesday: GOD'S COVENANT Deut. 30:1-20
Thursday: THE SONG OF MOSES Deut. 32:1-44
Friday: GOD'S BLESSINGS Deut. 33:1-29
Saturday: THE DEATH OF MOSES Deut. 34:1-12

Chapter 7

LET'S LOOK AT JOSHUA

JOSHUA PORTRAYS JESUS CHRIST,
CAPTAIN OF OUR SALVATION

MOBILIZATION OF THE ARMY (Joshua 1; 2)

Open your Bible to the text, Joshua 1; 2. We find the children of Israel right on the border of the land of promise, near the banks of the Jordan.

Joshua is the leader of the children of Israel now! Moses is dead! Joshua stands with bowed head and a lonely heart, for his wise counselor and friend has gone. But God spoke to him, *I will not fail thee, nor forsake thee. Be strong and of a good courage; be not afraid, neither be thou dismayed; for the LORD thy God is with thee withersoever thou goest* (Joshua 1:5,9).

We see both Joshua and the people prepared for the journey. Remember, Joshua had been one of the twelve spies who had been sent into Canaan forty years before. Now he sends two scouts to bring a report of the land. Read the story of Rahab and the spies in Joshua 2. Joshua asked them especially to find out the strength of Jericho, for this was the first stronghold they would have to attack after crossing the river.

We must know something of Canaan. The Canaanites, the people of the land, were the descendants of Canaan, the son of Ham. They were a wicked and idolatrous people. God had warned them in the destruction of Sodom and Gomorrah, but they had not changed a bit. Now God was going to destroy their power and give their land to the Israelites.

FORWARD MARCH (Joshua 3–5)

Read the story of this scene, Joshua 3–5.

Encouraged by the report the spies had brought, the Israelites removed from their encampment at Shittim, six miles from the Jordan, to a spot within a mile of the swollen stream. At dawn the officers passed through the camp and ordered all to watch the ark and follow it at a distance of two thousand cubits, *that ye may know the way by which ye must go: for ye have not passed this way heretofore* (Joshua 3:4). The great leader, Joshua, instructed the people to sanctify themselves, for on the morrow the Lord would do wonders among them. (See Joshua 3:5.)

The children of Israel had followed the cloud in the wilderness. Now they would follow the ark of the covenant which represented the presence of Jehovah.

At the beginning of the Exodus from Egypt there was a crossing of the Red Sea. And at the close of the Exodus, there was the crossing of the Jordan river. Both were most memorable events in the history of the children of Israel.

"Why didn't they go over the bridge?" a child questioned.

Because there were no bridges and only a few fords, and these not passable at this season of the year, the spies had no doubt crossed and recrossed by swimming. But how could a great host with women and children and baggage cross?

He gave the directions for the people to follow. Martin Luther said, "I know not the way He (Christ) leads me, but well do I know my Guide."

Joshua told the priests to take up the ark and step into the Jordan, when the river was overflowing all its banks. When the soles of their feet touched the waters of the Jordan, they stood on dry ground. (Joshua 3:9-17) This is impossible with men but with God all things are possible. God is always doing the impossible. "God's biddings are His enablings."

A negro once said, "If God tells me to jump through a stone wall, it would be my duty to jump; it would be God's duty to remove the wall!"

THE FALL OF JERICHO (Joshua 6)

A man, passing by a building which was being torn down, stopped to look at a laborer who was pulling on a rope fastened to the top of the wall.

"Do you think that you are going to pull that thick wall down that way?" he finally asked in amazement.

Between his tugs the man answered, "It doesn't look that way to me, but I guess the boss knows what he's about."

And the boss did know, for the wall had been undermined, and after an hour of tug after tug the great wall vibrated, swayed, and fell flat.

The walls of Jericho had to come down so that the Israelites might proceed to conquer the promised land,

PALESTINE
ISRAEL AND JUDAH

SIDON
TYRE
DAMASCUS
PHOENICIANS
DAN
KEDESH
ARAM

MEDITERRANEAN
SEA

MT. CARMEL
RIVER KISHON
MT. TABOR
SEA OF GALILEE
GOLAN?

WELL OF HAROD
VALLEY OF JEZREEL
BROOK CHERITH?
MT. GILBOA
ISRAEL
RAMOTH-GILEAD (RAMOTH)

SHECHEM
RIVER JORDAN
RIVER JABBOK

APHEK
PHILISTINES
EBENEZER?
SHILOH
BETHEL
AMMON

RAMAH
GILGAL
EKRON
GIBEAH
JERUSALEM
JERICHO
BEZER?
ASHDOD
BETH-SHEMESH
BETHLEHEM
MT. NEBO

ASHKELON
GATH?
TEKOA
HEBRON
MOAB
GAZA
EN-GEDI
JUDAH
DEAD SEA
GERAR?
ZIKLAG

BEERSHEBA

EDON SEIR

65

for Jericho was the key to southern Canaan. How could this be brought about? To the Israelites God's directions seemed strange, but like that laborer, they kept steadily at the part assigned them. They were confident that their Leader knew what they did not, and that they would soon enter the city. What was their task? Read Joshua 6.

The procession of priests, ark, men and trumpets, that marched around the city daily, were the only visible means for its capture. How futile must such a march have seemed to the people of Jericho, yes, to the Israelites themselves. But God knew what He would do.

Some would try to explain that the fall of Jericho was no miracle but a simple scientific fact. God knew that a certain vibration would destroy the wall. It was struck in the sound of the trumpet and shout and the wall fell.

Whether this is the case or not, the miracle remains that the wall fell. God accomplished the destruction with or without "scientific" means. The glory is God's, not Joshua's.

The fall of Jericho before the blast of Joshua's rams' horns was a miracle so stupendous that the rationalist can but discredit it. The Israelites believed that they were following God's plan. The seven trumpets, leading a procession seven days, and seven times on the seventh day, showed the Israelites that this was Jehovah's plan of conquest as directly as an American flag would inform people today that the property over which it waved was under the protection of the United States. God put an invisible band around the foundation of that city wall and tightened it, and when God does that to the foundation of any structure, national or personal—beware!

CAMPAIGN AT AI (Joshua 7; 8)

The capture of Jericho gave the Israelites a chance to enter central Canaan. The next place strategically important was Ai, which commanded the entrance into the valley leading into western Canaan.

As he had done in the case of Jericho, Joshua sent spies to Ai to learn the situation. Made over-confident by their recent success, they gave poor counsel on their return, saying, "Two or three thousand can go up and smite Ai. Let not all the people go up, for there are only a few." The small force was sent up the steep ascent, but when the garrison at Ai sallied forth and attacked them, the Israelites fled without striking a blow. In the disaster all saw the withdrawal of God's guiding hand. They soon learned that they could not trust in their own strength alone. *Not by might, nor by power, but by My Spirit, saith the Lord* (Zechariah 4:6).

One man's sin caused Israel's defeat. (Israel had become a nation and no one could act alone.) Achan had hidden the wedge of gold. Read the story in Joshua 7. Beware of the wedge of gold! (Joshua 7:13) Achan alone was guilty, yet we read: *Israel hath sinned, and they have also transgressed my covenant which I commanded them: for they have even taken of the accursed thing, and have also stolen, and dissembled also* (Joshua 7:11).

No one's sins affect himself alone. None of us liveth to himself. One stricken with smallpox can infect an entire schoolroom. A few influenza germs can infect a whole nation. The sin of one becomes the sin of the community.

Every sin you commit will hunt you down, find you out, and make you pay. Know this, there has never been one sin committed on this earth for which the man who committed it did not suffer. There was never a sin that paid. You may escape the law of man. You cannot escape the law of God.

SOUTHERN CAMPAIGN (Joshua 10)

The Israelites go out a second time to Ai. This time they are victors. The victory of Ai shows real military strategy. In working for the Lord there must always be a recognition of the value of the best in human reason, but strategy without obedience is worth nothing. Moody said, "Pray as if everything depended upon God and work as if everything depended upon you."

NORTHERN CAMPAIGN (Joshua 11)

After all of southern Canaan was in Israel's possession a new confederacy had to be faced and conquered. The northern kings had joined together and tried to break the power of the conquering Israelites. But in divine strength Joshua routed them all. This did not all happen at once. Scripture says that it took "a long time." At last the land rested from war. (Joshua 11:23)

Jerusalem was so named here for the first time in the Bible. To think that since then it has become possibly the most famous place in the world! The Crusaders shed rivers of blood trying to capture it. On a Sunday in 1917 General Allenby walked in with head uncovered and took this citadel without a sound of a cannon! It is a city with a great past history and although today it has little glory, its future history is brighter than any of its past. Here Christ will reign when He comes again in power and great glory. (Luke 21:27)

DIVISION OF THE LAND (Joshua 13–24)

Joshua was an old man now, about ninety years of age, and he realized that the conquest of the land was by no means complete. There yet remained "much land to be possessed." In order that the children of Israel might do this, he divided it among them.

"This is Judah's; this is Asher's; this is Simeon's; and this is Benjamin's," we hear the people saying as the scene opens. They said this even while the Amorites, the Jebusites, and the Hittites were in open possession of the promised land. (Joshua 13) The division made of the land was the announcement on faith of certain things which under God's guidance they proposed to realize by the long struggle which followed.

The strong did not take the best part of the land because they were strong, leaving the fragments for the weak, neither did the rich purchase the choicest spots, leaving the poor the more undesirable sites. They tried to determine God's will in the matter. God cares about distribution of goods.

Do you see any application of this principle today? God cares about the inequalities of condition of His children. He cares that the weak are thrust aside by the shrewd and strong. There is a will of God concerning all the questions of hours and wages, capital and labor. God is concerned in a more equal division of His blessings in this world. When He rules "everyone will sit under his own vine and fig tree."

CALEB'S POSSESSION (Joshua 14)

Caleb was eighty-five years old! Joshua and he were alone among the spies; they dared to trust God! How many spies did Moses send into Canaan? How many of their names can you remember? No doubt these two are the only ones. As a reward for their obedience, they were the only ones of all that generation who were permitted to enter Canaan eventually. (Numbers 14:24, 30; 26:65) Caleb asked his friend Joshua for the high and walled cities!

Caleb was old but he gloried in the hardness of the

task. One of Helen Keller's teachers said she was the happiest person she had ever met, even though she was deaf, dumb and blind. Her teacher attributed it to her having to overcome so much. Caleb was the happiest man in the camp because he had overcome so much and yet had fields to conquer!

Horace Mann said, "Difficulties are things which show what men are."

The Lord has never promised His children that they will have an easy time serving Him. In fact Christ said, *In the world ye shall have tribulation* (John 16:33). The promise is not for ease; the promise is for victory. Christ says, *I have overcome the world.* We grow in adversity for we learn to trust the Lord more.

Paul said to Timothy, *Endure hardness, as a good soldier of Jesus Christ* (II Timothy 2:3).

JOSHUA'S FAREWELL (Joshua 24)

Joshua had become an old man. He knew that he could not live much longer. He wanted to give the people some last words of admonition.

He called first the leaders and then all the people together and urged them to remember the power and faithfulness of God and admonished them to be faithful to Him. "Now therefore fear the Lord, and serve Him." He warned them against apostasy. He said, *Choose you this day whom ye will serve; whether the gods which your fathers served that were on the other side of the flood, or the gods of the Amorites . . .* Then he added, *As for me and my house, we will serve the Lord* (Joshua 24:15).

It is a good thing to have people make an open confession and commit themselves to a solemn promise. These older men who had made an open confession were true to their promises.

It is a great help for young people to stand and make

a public confession of Christ and unite with the church. You have made a definite commitment which gives you something to live up to. See what Paul says about confession, Romans 10:9,10.

The people said that day, "Nay: but we will serve the Lord."

At one hundred and ten years of age the grand old man, Joshua, died. The book closes with death. We see three graves. Joshua's, the great leader of Israel; Eleazer's, the priest; and Joseph's, whose bones the children of Israel had carried with them from Egypt and which were now buried in the land of promise.

Here is a great tribute to a great leader, *And Israel served the Lord all the days of Joshua* (Joshua 24:31).

THINK AND DO

Today we are faced with choices of every kind. Name some that we must make—education, vocation, friendships, and others.

Joshua asked the people to make a very important choice. What was it? (Joshua 24:14,15)

Is one religion just as good as another? Why are you a Christian?

What gods are people asked to serve today? (Money, pleasure, position, self, etc.)

Joshua was a leader of courage. Underline the word "courage" in chapter 1.

INFORMATION PLEASE

1. **Why did God tell Joshua to destroy the Canaanites?**
2. **What result followed because Israel allowed some of the Canaanites to remain in the land and failed to obey God?**
3. **Why did God spare Rahab when she was such a wicked woman?**
4. **Why had not the Israelites entered the Promised Land 40 years earlier?**

Minimum Daily Requirements / Spiritual Vitamins

Sunday: JOSHUA'S COMMISSION Joshua 1; 2
Monday: CROSSING THE JORDAN Joshua 3
Tuesday: THE FALL OF JERICHO Joshua 6
Wednesday: THE SIN OF ACHAN Joshua 7
Thursday: OCCUPATION OF THE LAND Joshua 11
Friday: CALEB'S POSSESSION Joshua 14
Saturday: JOSHUA'S FAREWELL Joshua 24

Chapter 8

LET'S LOOK AT JUDGES and RUTH

JESUS CHRIST, OUR DELIVERER JUDGE,
OUR KINSMAN-REDEEMER

Someone has called the Book of Judges the account of the Dark Ages of the Israelitish people. The people forsook God (Judges 2:13) and God forsook the people. (Judges 2:23)

Judges covers the period after the death of their great leader, Joshua, to the ascension of Saul to the throne of Israel. The people were ruled by judges whom God raised up to deliver His oppressed people. We read, *In those days there was no king in Israel* (Judges 17:6). It covers the history of about the first three hundred and fifty years in the land of promise. It is a record of great exploits.

There are fifteen judges—Othniel, Ehud, Shamgar, Deborah, Barak, Gideon, Tola, Jair, Jephthah, Ibzan, Elon, Abdon, Samson, Eli and Samuel. (Abimelech was not called of God to judge.)

The chief judges were Deborah, Gideon, Samson and Samuel.

There is a phrase running through the whole book— *Every man did that which was right in his own eyes* (Judges 17:6). Mark this phrase every time you find it. We find the people falling away from Jehovah and worshiping the gods of the nations round about them. (Judges 2:13) They forgot that God had chosen them for a purpose—to tell the world the truth that there is but one true God. In punishment for their sins God would deliver them into the hand of that nation. Then under the oppression of these new enemies they would cry to God for mercy and He would hear them and send a judge to deliver them. And so the book is full of rebellion, punishment, misery, and deliverance. It has a minor key throughout.

Professor Moorehead, D.D., gives an outline for Judges which is easy to remember. "Seven apostasies, seven servitudes to seven heathen nations, seven deliverances!"

We read of man's constant failure and God's constant mercy.

Read this book this week. Don't regard this as a severe task. It can be done in an hour or two.

To learn just the great facts of the Bible, however necessary it is, will never satisfy the Christian and make him a real blessing to others. We must know what God is teaching us in each book.

ISRAEL'S FAILURE (Judges 1—3:4)

Joshua had died. (Judges 1:1) Much of the promised land must be conquered. The first act of the children of Israel was to seek God's will as to how they should commence the final conquest. They began well. They consulted God.

God appointed Judah, the kingly tribe. (Judges 1:2) The work began in earnest but it ended in weakness. The people did not obey God.

Israel's troubles were due directly to her disobedience to God. They did not exterminate the enemies in the land but rather worshiped the idols of the people and became corrupted in their morals.

The children of Israel went into the land and settled where they wanted and began to raise enough for their living. Soon an enemy would come along, catch the tribe off guard, and take the people captive. Their enemies were "fifth columnists" within. God had told His people to do away with them.

Sometimes we wonder why God didn't remove all the enemies from the promised land before He let the children of Israel go in. But God had a definite reason. (Read Judge 3:1-4.) *Now these are the nations which the Lord left, to prove Israel . . . to know whether they would hearken unto the commandments of the LORD.*

God wanted the chosen people to realize that they were a holy people. They must not mix with the wicked nations about them. They must continually separate themselves. God knew that separation makes men strong. Christians today must remember that they cannot mix with the world. They must keep close to God and war against sin and unrighteousness. God wants us to be good warriors. Read Ephesians 6:10-18 and see the armor He provides. Our world today is full of deadly Canaanites.

And so we see that a false toleration toward a people

so utterly corrupt resulted in the undoing of God's chosen people. See the result of this disobedience, Judges 2:20-22.

THE JUDGES (Judges 3:5–16:31)

This scene gives us the picture of seven failures, seven servitudes and seven deliverances. The Israelites intermarried with the heathen, worshiped at their shrines, and practiced their vices.

First Oppression, Judges 3:7-11
        Sin—Idolatry
        Punishment—Eight years
        Deliverer and Judge—Othniel

Second Oppression, Judges 3:12-31
        Sin—Immorality and idolatry
        Punishment—Eighteen years
        Deliverers and Judges—Ehud and Shamgar

Third Oppression, Judges 4; 5
        Sin—Departed from God
        Punishment—Twenty years
        Deliverers and Judges—Deborah and Barak

Fourth Oppression, Judges 6–8:32
        Sin—Departed from God
        Punishment—Midianites for seven years
        Deliverer and Judge—Gideon

Fifth Oppression, Judges 8:33–10:5
        Sin—Departed from God
        Punishment—Civil war, etc.
        Deliverers and Judges—Tola and Jair

Sixth Oppression, Judges 10:6–12:15
        Sin—Idolatry increased
        Punishment—Philistines and Ammonites, eighteen years
        Deliverers and Judges—Jephthah (and successors)

Seventh Oppression, Judges 13–16
    Sin—Departed from God
    Punishment—Philistines, forty years
    Deliverer and Judge—Samson

Joshua had no successor. After his death, each tribe acted independently. There was no capital and no fixed government.

There was no unity of action except in the time of danger, when the tribes combined for their own good. When the people sinned against God, their enemies defeated them and ruled them. When in their distress they sought the Lord, He sent great leaders called judges, who delivered them. The outline just given shows you the record of sin and servitude.

But this scene is not only filled with servitude, it also records deliverances, for God was always near His people and when they cried He answered. God is always brooding over His disobedient children. He promises us that He will never leave us nor forsake us. We see defeat on man's part; but deliverance on God's part. *Where sin abounded, grace did much more abound* (Romans 5:20).

FIRST APOSTASY — (Judges 3:7–11)

We find the Israelites settling among the Syrian nations. They seemed too ready to live at peace with these other nations and to yield not a little for the sake of peace. (Read the few verses 3:5-8 to see what they did.) They intermarried to make their position safer. They traded with the Amorites, Hivites, Perizzites. They determined on boundary lines to make things run smoothly. Next they accepted their neighbor's religion (Judges 3:7), and then his bad customs. But soon the Mesopotamians began to oppress them. (Judges 3:8) The Israelites then realized that they had a God from whom they had departed. Israel was a prodigal people.

They had left the God whose presence before had assured them victory. For eight years they were under the oppression of these northern nations. Year by year conditions grew worse.

It was from the far south that God sent help in answer to their pitiful cry. (Judges 3:9) The deliverer was Othniel, who was Caleb's nephew. No doubt he had had frequent skirmishes with the Arab marauders from the wilderness. *The Spirit of the Lord came upon him, and he judged Israel, and went out to war* (Judges 3:10). He prayed first, then went out to battle. When we see an army bow in prayer, as the Swiss did at Morat, the Scots at Bannockburn, and General Mac-Arthur's troops in the Philippines, we have faith in their spirit and courage for they are feeling their dependence on God!

Othniel's first concern was to put away the idolatry of Israel and teach them the law of the Lord and remind them of their calling as a nation. Soon success and victory were theirs. (Judges 3:10-11)

Othniel, the first of the judges, was one of the best. He pointed Israel to a higher level of reverence for God and His plans. Forty years of rest followed.

No man can do real service for his country who does not fear God and love righteousness more than country.

SECOND APOSTASY — (Judges 3:12-31)

God used different kinds of men to deliver His people. Israel's second judge, Ehud, is in marked contrast to Othniel, the judge without reproach.

The long peace which the country enjoyed after the Mesopotamian army had been driven out let the people fall into spiritual weakness. (Judges 3:12) This time the Moabites led the attack. The punishment lasted for eighteen years. Again, the people cried to God, and Ehud, with whom Shamgar's name is associated, was the deliverer. (Judges 3:15) This left-handed Benjamite chose his own method of action and assassinated the Moabite king. His crime is one that "stinks in our nostrils." But eighty years of rest for Israel followed. (Judges 3:30)

Shamgar, the man of the ox-goad, follows in line. (Judges 3:31)

THIRD APOSTASY — (Judges 4; 5)

Now a prophetess arises in Israel. (Judges 4:4) She was one of those rare women whose heart burns with enthusiasm when men's hearts are despondent. Many a queen has reigned with honor and wisdom, and often a woman's voice has struck a note which has aroused nations.

Israel had been oppressed for twenty years. (Judges 4:3) The oppression was terrible under Sisera. Again they cried and God heard. This time the story of deliverance was filled with romance and song. Deborah, the daughter of the people, had gained the confidence of the people to such a degree that they had appointed her as judge.

Deborah called Barak to help her. Together they delivered Israel from their oppression. The land had been so filled with Canaanite spoilers that the highways could not be used. War was everywhere and the Israelites were defenseless and crushed, but God delivered them.

In the Chicago University, in the Oriental Institute, there is a wonderful exhibit of ivory and gold ornaments which were found in 1937 in a palace of the prince of Megiddo of the thirteenth century B.C. This is just the time when Barak was judge. Here we see the personal belongings of one of the Canaanite princes who oppressed Israel with nine hundred chariots of iron.

FOURTH APOSTASY — (Judges 6–8:32)

But a fourth apostasy came. (Read Judges 6:1.) This time the deliverer was Gideon, a humble farmer. The Midianites had held the Israelites under bondage for seven years. So terrible was it that the people hid themselves in caves and dens and were hunted in the mountains. (Judges 6:2) Again they cried unto the Lord. Gideon was called to act as deliverer. He broke down the altar of Baal and restored the worship of God. The story of the conflict is one of the most fascinating in history. Everyone knows the story of Gideon and his band of three hundred with their pitchers and horns. Read the story. (Judges 7:7-24)

After the great victory over the Midianites, they sought to make Gideon king. He refused. Gideon was not perfect. We find in the record some things that he should not have done, but he did have a faith in Jehovah that God could honor, and He gave his name a place in the Hall of Faith in Hebrews 11.

No doubt you all have heard of the band of men called "Gideons." Years ago two or three Christian traveling men banded themselves together and decided they would put Bibles in hotel rooms. This small band has grown into thousands, until now, there are Bibles in hotel rooms all over the United States. These Gideons do not fight with steel swords but with the Sword of the Spirit.

In 1926-28 excavations were made by Xenia Seminary and the American School under the direction of Melvin Grove Kyle and Albright. They found in a city built by Othniel (1500 B.C.) many hidden grain pits, showing how insecure life and property were in the days when there was no organized defense against the Midianites who made constant raids upon the Israelites. The people took refuge in dens and caves.

FIFTH APOSTASY — (Judges 8:33–10:5)

A fifth time we see the people falling into the sin of idolatry by worshiping the Baalim almost immediately upon the death of Gideon. The record is: *As soon as Gideon was dead, that the children of Israel turned again, and went a whoring after Baalim* (Judges 8:33). How often the personal influence of the hero is everything while he is alive but confusion follows on his death.

SIXTH APOSTASY — (Judges 10:6–12:15)

In the sixth apostasy we find the people almost entirely given over to idolatry. Their condition was appalling. God sent judgment this time from the Philistines for eighteen years. At last, sorely distressed, they cried to God. For the first time it is recorded that He refused to hear them and reminded them of how repeatedly He had delivered them. (Judges 10:13) The true attitude of Jehovah toward them is found in this statement—*His soul was grieved for the misery of Israel* (Judges 10:16).

Deliverance came through Jephthah. The Hebrews have always produced men of a passionate religious fervor. The Arab of the present day is much the same. He can be excited to a holy war in which thousands perish. With the battle cry of Allah and his Prophet, he forgets fear. He is both fierce and generous. He rises to great faith, then sinks to earthly passions. We have the type in Deborah, David, Elijah and Jephthah. Jephthah's history is full of interest. He was a man of heroic daring. Read the story of his vows and victories, especially the vow that he made concerning his only child. (Judges 11:30-40) After his victory, Jephthah judged Israel but six years.

SEVENTH APOSTASY — (Judges 13–16)

The seventh apostasy opens with the words *Israel did evil again in the sight of the LORD* (Judges 13:1). This time they were disciplined by the Philistines under whose awful oppression they lived for forty years. Here we read the story of Samson. It is a story filled with opportunity and failure. This man was appointed of God before birth, to deliver Israel from the Philistines. (Judges 13:5)

In those days everything was dependent upon physical strength. That was what made a leader great. In this case God used it to begin the deliverance from the Philistines. Everything should have been in Samson's favor, but he entered into an unholy alliance which meant his downfall. The final fall occurred at Gaza. (Read Judges 16.) Nothing is more pathetic than Samson, blind and bound, grinding in the house of the Philistines, when he ought to have been delivering his nation from them. (Judges 16:20, 21)

The story ends with Samson and is taken up in I Samuel. The remaining chapters, and the Book of Ruth, have their chronological place in this period.

THE APPENDIX — (Judges 17–21)

These last chapters give us a picture of anarchy and confusion. Israel had forsaken God and now we see the depths into which they had sunk. Read Judges 17:6 and you will find the reason for it all.

The story of God's children is full of wanderings and returnings, bondage and deliverances. Christ is our Judge and Deliverer. Let us obey!

THE BOOK OF RUTH

This delightful story should be read in connection with the first chapters of Judges as, no doubt, it gives us an idea of the domestic life in Israel at that period of anarchy.

Ruth was the great-grandmother of David. This book establishes the lineage of David, the ancestor of Christ. It tells of the beginning of the Messianic family, within the Messianic nation into which over a thousand years later the Messiah was to be born.

There are some interesting things to notice in this book. Ruth was a Moabitess. These people were descendants of Lot. They were heathen. God, in establishing the family which was to produce the world's Saviour, chose a beautiful heathen girl, led her to Bethlehem and made her the bride of Boaz. This is God's grace. He adopts the Gentiles into Christ's family. Of course, we know that although Ruth was born a heathen, through her first husband, or Naomi, she learned of the true God. She left her idols and her people and chose to serve the living God.

Boaz was the son of Rahab, the harlot found in Jericho. See Matthew 1:5. So we see that David's great-grandmother was a Moabitess and his great-grandfather was half Canaanite.

THINK AND DO

Israel had come from long bondage in Egypt and forty years of wandering in the wilderness to the Promised Land. How did they meet this new adjustment in living?

Compare the way Israel met the hardships in their new land with the early Puritans who came to America.

For what purpose had God chosen Israel?

How has this faith in one true God been the foundation of our Christian civilization?

Why does God allow His children to encounter hardships and dangers?

Can we be tolerant toward people today who are deliberately opposed to God as the Canaanites were of old? What do you think God's command to us would be?

One of the common sins of Israel was intermarriage with the Canaanites. What is your opinion about dating those of other faiths? Do you think it would be wise never to date a person who is not a Christian? Can you think of any Scripture to illustrate your point?

Should a Protestant date a Catholic? Remember, if a Protestant marries a Catholic, he or she must give up his religious faith, be married by a priest, promise to raise their children as Catholics. There can be no fellowship between Catholics and non-Catholics. These marriages of different faiths almost always end up in tragedies.

Another of Israel's sins was mixing with the wicked nations and worshiping their idols. Does creed (what we believe) affect our conduct? Was this true with Israel?

What great woman was a judge? (Judges 4; 5) Are women leaders today? In what fields may the young women serve?

God calls men from all walks of life. Can we have a call from God for full time Christian service and still be in business, in industry, in teaching, etc.? How can you be a Christian business man; a Christian surgeon?

Why did Samson fail? Lack of character always means failure in every walk of life. What are the temptations today that take away the strength of youth —such as drinking, gambling, low moral standards, unwholesome sex relationships, disrespect of parents, lack of prayer and Bible study, etc.?

Minimum Daily Requirements / Spiritual Vitamins

Sunday: ONLY PARTIAL VICTORIES Judges 1–2:5

Monday: INSTITUTION OF THE JUDGES Judges 2:16–3:11

Tuesday: DEBORAH AND BARAK Judges 4:4–5:31

Wednesday: GIDEON, THE FARMER Judges 6:1-16; 7:16-25

Thursday: JEPHTHAH'S TERRIBLE VOW Judges 11:12-40

Friday: SAMSON, THE STRONG MAN Judges 15 and 16

Saturday: THE STORY OF RUTH Book of Ruth

Chapter 9

LET'S LOOK AT I SAMUEL

*I SAMUEL PORTRAYS JESUS CHRIST,
OUR KING*

Kingdom history begins with the Book of Samuel. The long period of the rule of the judges ends with Samuel. When Samuel came into power, the people were in an awful state. They had practically rejected God and we hear them clamoring for an earthly king. (I Samuel 8:4-7) This book begins the five hundred year period of Israel's kings (1095-586 B.C.)

Samuel — Saul — David

The book may be divided under the names of three of its chief characters—Samuel (1–7), Saul (8–15), and David (16–31). The history of this book is presented to us in the attractive cloak of biography. Everyone likes a true story.

We all have known and loved the stories recorded in I Samuel from the time we were little children. Who does not know the story of the boy Samuel (chapter 3), and David and Goliath (17), and the friendship of David and Jonathan (18).

This book, of course, is named for its most prominent figure, Samuel. Probably he wrote the greater part of it, through chapter 24. Nathan and Gad finished it. (I Chron. 29:29 and I Samuel 10:25)

SAMUEL, THE KING MAKER (I Samuel 1–7)

Samuel—"asked of God!" That is the meaning of his name. This book opens with the record of Hannah, Samuel's mother, praying for a son whom God could use. Samuel, the last of the judges, was God's answer to this prayer. *But Samuel ministered before the Lord, being a child* (I Samuel 2:18).

Throughout Samuel's long and useful life, he was God's man. He was pre-eminently a man of prayer. This first book which bears his name is a marvelous study of the place and power of prayer, illustrated from life. He was a child of prayer (I Sam. 3:1-19); he brought victory to his people through prayer (7:5-10); when the nation wanted a king, Samuel prayed unto the Lord (8:6); intercessory prayer was the keynote of his life. (I Samuel 12:19-23)

It was in the dark and troublous times of Israel that we hear the prayer of faith from the lips of a simple, trusting woman, Hannah. She asked God for a son whom she could dedicate to Him for service. (I Sam. 1:9-19)

When Samuel was born, Hannah brought him to the tabernacle at Shiloh. Although the corruption of the priesthood was appalling, **Samuel was protected and** grew as a boy in the fear of the Lord. (I Samuel 1:24-28; 2:12-26; 3:1-21)

Eli was both judge and priest at this time. He had ruled for forty years. He was an indulgent father and his two sons, Hophni and Phinehas, also priests, were allowed to act in a most disgraceful manner. As a result there was moral corruption and God warned Eli of the downfall of his house.

Fungus growth in a tree usually is not detected for a long time. Everything seems right outwardly, but when the crash suddenly comes, the state of the tree is seen. Israel had been sinning for a long time. At length the catastrophe came in the disaster recorded at this time. (I Samuel 4)

During the next invasion of their enemies, the Philistines, Israel was defeated, the ark was taken and Eli's sons were killed. When Eli heard all this, the old man, now ninety-eight years of age, died of the shock. (I Samuel 4)

We cannot win while we war against God! There can be no peace in our own heart, or in a nation, when individuals and nations are not surrendered to the mastery of Jesus Christ our Lord.

Apart from the immediate causes, rebellion against God is the root reason for tragic wars today. Civilization, in general, has not been seeking first and always the glory and will of God. The United States has failed to meet this test, as well as all the other nations. Civilized nations have failed, as they were bound to do, and they always will fail as long as God is left out.

Though this life is bound to be a fight, it may always be a winning fight if we enlist under the banner of the Captain of our Salvation and make His will our will. *We are more than conquerors* (Romans 8:37).

After Israel's first defeat by the Philistines, did they

do right or not by looking to the ark of God for protection? (I Samuel 4:3-7,10)

The ark of God was a very poor substitute for the God of the ark. Many people think that when they wear religious symbols, or perform religious rituals, or give money to charitable causes that they will be safe. They think that these things are a charm, or talisman, to bring them victory. Can you give some illustrations of this?

Samuel was the last of the judges, the first of the prophets, and the founder of the monarchy. Beside this, he started a school of the prophets, a kind of seminary. The record of this great man's life is beyond reproach. It is hard to find a single mistake that Samuel made.

And the Lord appeared again in Shiloh (I Sam. 3:21). God revisited Shiloh! For Shiloh had been left. Read Judges 21:19-21. The place of worship had been turned into a place of feasting and dancing. Shiloh was the location of the house of God from the days of Joshua to Samuel. David moved it to Jerusalem. The ark was removed by the Philistines in Samuel's childhood and from then on Shiloh ceased to be of great importance. (I Samuel 4:3,11)

What brought the revival? Three things:

1. A praying mother, chapter 1.
2. A chastened people, chapter 2.
3. A faithful prophet, chapter 3.

We need a praying band of Christians, a people brought to a sense of their need, and a consecrated preacher to bring about revival.

Under the Philistine rule Israel had no definite center of worship. Samuel grew into manhood and assumed the leadership for which he had been born. The first hopeful sign after Israel's long rebellion and defeat was that they had a sense of need. They began to want God. They "lamented after Jehovah." The Jews are going to do this again some day (Zechariah 12:10,11) when Christ "whom they have pierced" returns to this earth and reveals Himself to His own people.

God cannot do much for people who do not feel that they need anything. God pities that person. There are those who think they are "all right."

"Well," said Samuel, "if you really mean business, you've got to show me. Do something. Prove it. How? Put away your strange gods." (See I Sam. 7:3) "Put away" might be translated "cut it out." If you mean business, God will mean business. Religion is not just a matter of emotion but also of the will.

Someone has said that there are two reasons why we are afraid to open our heart's door and let Christ come in. (Rev. 3:20) We are afraid of what He will cast out of our lives, or of what He will bring in. Look into your own heart and see if this is true.

In just a brief paragraph we find the actual story of Samuel's judgeship. His home was at Ramah. From here he was a circuit rider covering his territory once a year to Bethel, Gilgal and Mizpeh, and overseeing and administering the affairs of the people. (I Sam. 7:15-17) We find missionaries doing this today. They choose some place as home center and then move out through the surrounding country.

Samuel established a school for the prophets at his home in Ramah. This was the beginning of the "order" of the prophets, or seers. When the ark was taken, the priests were scattered. This is when Samuel retired to his home in Ramah. Through Samuel, God introduced a new way of dealing with Israel. He called prophets through whom He could speak. It was with Samuel that prophecy became a definite part of the life of Israel. Samuel gathered groups about him called "Sons of the Prophets." They were found in Shiloh, Gilgal, Bethel, Samaria and Ramah. (See Acts 3:24.)

Samuel's greatest ministry was the organization of the kingdom. The independent tribes were now going to be formed into a nation. In order to survive among other strong nations, Israel must become powerful. They had refused to take God seriously and obey Him as He had commanded them, so He permitted Samuel to find a king for them. The people wanted to be *"like* all the nations." God wanted them to be *unlike* the other nations. In Deuteronomy 17:14-20 God had prophesied that Israel should have a king but He did not want them to become independent of Him.

SAUL, THE KING CHOSEN (I Samuel 8–15)

God never intended Israel to have any king but Himself. He would send them great leaders and these in turn would receive their orders directly from Him. But Israel, in her falling away, had become restless. They wanted a king like the other surrounding nations. We find God granting their request. Here is a great lesson. We either can have God's best or His second best—His directive or His permissive will.

God always give us the best we will take, "for His mercy endureth forever." We are free human agents. We can choose for ourselves; but we may well tremble at the consequences. We must choose God's best or our own way.

Saul, their first king, was a failure. He was handsome to look at, he was tall and of a noble mien. He started out splendidly. He proved to be an able military leader. He defeated the enemies about him—the Philistines, the Amalekites and the Ammonites.

Saul was humble at first, but we find him becoming proud and disobedient to God. No man had a greater opportunity than Saul and no man ever was a greater failure. His jealousy of David bordered on insanity.

Saul was not right with God so he was not right anywhere!

Saul had marvelous gifts and privileges. We watch him gain his spurs. We see that men may have a good beginning but if heady and stiffnecked they end in failure.

On the walls of an old temple was found this picture: a king forging from his crown a chain, and near by a slave making of his chain a crown, and underneath was written, "Life is what man makes of it, no matter of what it is made."

All through the years Samuel mourned for Saul. When he failed, Samuel was faithful in warning him, then in loneliness he mourned over him. Multiplied verses tell the story. (I Samuel 15:35.)

In a battle with the Philistines, Saul and his three sons met death. Here a life so full of promise ended in defeat and failure. Saul had not obeyed God absolutely. For instance, if I should sell one thousand acres of land and would reserve one acre in the center, I would have the right to go over those one thousand acres to get to mine. One trouble with us is that we reserve a room for Satan in our hearts and he knows he has his right-of-way. This was the trouble with Saul.

Think of the difference between the end of Saul of Tarsus (Paul) and Saul the king! One put God first, the other himself!

God is showing in this book that He must be all in all; that His children have no blessing apart from Him.

DAVID, THE KING, PROVEN (I Samuel 16—31)

As the third division of the book opens we see Samuel mourning for Saul. God rebukes him and tells him to arise and anoint the new king. (I Samuel 16:1)

David, "the apple of God's eye," was one of the greatest characters of all times. He made great contributions to the history of Israel spiritually and nationally.

In this book we see David as a shepherd lad, a minstrel, an armor-bearer, a captain, the king's son-in-law, a writer of psalms, and a fugitive. He was anointed three times and was to be the founder of the royal line of which the King of kings came—Christ.

David, Jesse's son and the great-grandson of Ruth and Boaz, was born in Bethlehem. He was the youngest of eight sons. When David was only eighteen, God told Samuel to anoint him king to succeed Saul. As a boy he tended his father's sheep and we read of his brave deeds in defending them from wild beasts.

As a harpist, David's fame reached the King. Saul's melancholy caused him to be called into the court to play. One of the most charming stories of real love in friendship is found between David and Jonathan, Saul's son.

When David was promoted to a high command in the army, his great success roused the jealousy of Saul who determined to kill him. He made five attacks on David's life. (See I Samuel 19:10,15,20.) But God preserved David. *If God be for us, who can be against us* (Romans 8:31)? David was delivered from all these dangers. Read David's words in Psalm 59. Read Psalm 37.

These were trying days for the young man David who had been appointed to the kingly office. It was natural that he should go to Samuel for protection. All this was training for the one whom God was preparing for the throne.

He not only learned how to know and handle men but how to handle himself. He became independent and courageous. He learned, too, in those trying days, to trust God, not men. He always awaited God's time.

He was an outcast for no wrong that he had done

but because of the insane jealousy of Saul. He grew under his trials and afflictions. Instead of letting Saul's hatred harden his heart, he returned love for hate.

He learned to be a warrior those days, too. He was to become the head of a great nation and God was training him for active service.

Finally David took refuge in flight. During this time Samuel died. Twice was Saul's life in David's hand but both times he spared Saul. Feeling that he should "perish one day by the hand of Saul," he took refuge among the Philistines. Psalm 56 was written. After Saul and his sons were killed by the Philistines David's exile ended.

The closing chapter of our book is draped in black. It gives the closing picture of one of the most disastrous failures. Saul died on the field of battle by his own hand. Advantages and opportunities in youth never guarantee success in manhood. One must keep true to God. Saul's undoing was not so much disobedience, as half-hearted obedience. (I Samuel 15) He was a victim of human pride and jealousy.

THINK AND DO

I Samuel begins with the birth of Samuel and ends with the death of Saul. Compare Samuel and Saul.

Follow Saul's rise and fall. What were his weaknesses? What was his strength?

What made Saul "fumble the ball" in the game of life? Follow it carefully.

Test yourself: Saul lived in an atmosphere of unrest. Israel was surrounded by her enemies, the Philistines and Ammonites. Saul had not found his rest in God. You are living in a restless, upset age, filled with fear and chaos. Do you not find yourself jittery and restless? Do you have to have the radio going while you are reading and working? Do you feel that you have to be doing something all the time? Do you enjoy being alone? Are you mentally and spiritually healthy? What will keep you happy as a Christian?

Discuss the difference between the end of Saul of Tarsus (Paul) and Saul the king. What was the secret of the difference?

Minimum Daily Requirements / Spiritual Vitamins

Sunday: SAMUEL, "ASKED OF GOD" I Samuel 1–3

Monday: SAMUEL, THE PROPHET I Samuel 4–7

Tuesday: SAUL, THE KING I Samuel 8–12

Wednesday: SAUL, THE SELF-WILLED I Samuel 13–15

Thursday: DAVID ANOINTED I Samuel 16–18

Friday: DAVID'S ADVENTURES I Samuel 19; 20; 22; 24

Saturday: DEATH OF SAMUEL AND SAUL I Samuel 25; 26; 31

Chapter 10

LET'S LOOK AT II SAMUEL

*II SAMUEL PORTRAYS JESUS CHRIST,
OUR KING*

We must not only crown Christ as King of our life,
but we must set Him on His rightful throne.

The first Book of Samuel records the failure of man's
king, Saul. Second Samuel describes the enthronement
of God's king, David, and the establishment of the
"House of David" through which the Messiah, Jesus
Christ, should later come. When Christ comes again,
He will sit upon the throne of David. (Isaiah 9:7; Luke
1:32)

The Book of Second Samuel is occupied with the
story of David as king. (II Sam. 5:3) It does not tell

the whole story for it begins with I Samuel and runs into I Kings. I Chronicles deals with it from another standpoint.

It will make it easy to remember the contents of this book if we study it as a biography. David now occupies the field of view. He comes into his own. Let us begin with I Samuel 16.

The story of David the shepherd is found in I Samuel 16 and 17; then we see him as a prince in the court, I Samuel 18–20; and finally as an exile in chapters 21–31.

There is no one found anywhere in God's Word who is more versatile. He is David, the shepherd boy, the court musician, the soldier, the true friend, the outcast captain, the king, the great general, the loving father, the poet, the sinner, the brokenhearted old man, but always the lover of God. We find him as a sort of Robin Hood of the Bible. We love the stories of his daring courage, his encounters with lions, bears and the giant.

He was a man of wonderful personal power and charm. Can you find, as you read this book, the record that portrays the following qualities which stand out so clearly?

1. Faithfulness, 2. Modesty, 3. Patience, 4. Courage, 5. Big-heartedness, 6. Trustfulness, 7. Penitence.

Why are we assured of David's success when he is made king? Saul chose the way of self; David chose God's way. Because of this, God called him a "man after His own heart." Notice after Saul's death David made no effort to seize the kingdom by force. Even after Judah claimed him as their king, it was seven years before Israel crowned him. David knew that it was God's plan that he should be king of Israel but he was willing to wait.

Michelangelo once said of a piece of marble, "I see an angel in that marble and I must get him out." God was shaping David. He saw a king in a shepherd lad. It took some time to chisel out a king, but we find here, as always, it pays to wait God's time.

DAVID'S RISE — SUPREMACY AND RULE
(II Samuel 1-10)

As this scene opens we find David just returning to Ziklag after his great victory over the Amalekites. He had come back weary in body but refreshed in spirit because of his great success. No doubt he was wondering what had been the outcome of that great battle at Mount Gilboa. His dearest friends, Jonathan and King Saul, were in that battle.

David was not kept in suspense long. An Amalekite, from the camp of Israel, came running that great distance, Bedouin style, to tell David of the disaster. No doubt the story the messenger told was made up and David dealt severely with him. (Read II Samuel 1:1-16.)

David was now just thirty (II Sam. 5:4) and never did a man at that age, or any age, act in a nobler way. His generous heart not only forgot all that Saul had done but remembered all that was favorable in Saul's character. Recall some of the things Saul had done against David.

How beautiful is this spirit of forgiveness! See that spirit when men nailed Christ to a tree (Luke 23:34), and when men stoned a martyr to death (Acts 7:60). David wrote a song for this occasion called "The Song of the Bow." It is filled with extreme tenderness when it speaks of his friend. (II Sam. 1:19-27)

David inquired of God where he should set up his kingdom, and God told him in Hebron. No sooner had David gone up to the city than the men of Judah came, and anointed him king over the house of Judah. Although it was not all that God had promised David, it was a large installment, for Judah was the imperial tribe. (II Samuel 2:1-11)

David's start was slow and discouraging. But David had faith in God. He was patient and was willing to wait for God to lead. He was humble before God and man.

Shall we not all adopt David's plan of life? He started right! He began with God. He committed every plan into His keeping. (Psalm 37:5) David never forgot that God was supreme. When he sinned, he bowed in penitence and sorrow and God forgave him.

In the prime of his life, at thirty years of age, David entered upon his complete inheritance. He reigned forty years in all, including seven and one-half years in Hebron over Judah and thirty-three years in Jerusalem over the whole land. The fortress of Jerusalem was still in the hands of the Canaanites but was captured early in David's reign. (II Samuel 5:6-10)

One of the great results of David's kingship was the unity of the whole nation under him as leader. He brought the various conflicting elements into one group. We find a united people under a young leader united to God. The Hebrews needed only to have kept on following David's leading down the years to have gone on from greatness to greatness. They had only to follow David's greater Son to have gone on from glory to glory!

He trusted God with all his heart and leaned not to his own understanding. He acknowledged God in all his ways and God did direct his path. (Proverbs 3:6) How did David obtain guidance? By asking for it. Just how God gave the answer we are not told. God has assured us that if we ask He will answer. (I John 5:14,15; Jer. 33:3) God never breaks His word. We have to make decisions almost every hour of our life. Shall I continue this course in my life? Shall my vacation be spent at home, traveling, at rest? Would we take false steps if He made the decisions for us?

What place in life has God in mind for you?

Do you believe that He has a definite purpose for you? If so, how are you going to find out what it is?

What was the greatest thing David did for his people?

He captured Jerusalem, built it bigger and stronger, conquered the Philistines and unified the people. But all this would be of little use without putting God at the center. This is really what gave the nation unity and power. Neither a nation nor an individual can be great without Christ in its heart.

All the events in David's reign that followed the capture of Jerusalem may be summed up in these words, *David waxed greater and greater: for the LORD of hosts was with him* (I Chron. 11:9). God had been getting David ready for this reign. Training is difficult. You know, "It is good to bear the yoke in youth." Many a great man can testify to this.

David was an active man. He was fond of work. His wars with outside nations had ceased. Now he sought to find what he could do to improve and beautify his kingdom. He compared the elegance of his own palace with the tabernacle where Jehovah dwelt. He thought this difference ought not to be. He called Nathan, the prophet, and consulted him about building a temple for Jehovah. At first, it seemed as if God would let him do this, but God had a different purpose for David. Read what God told Nathan to tell to David. (II Samuel 7:4-17)

God told Nathan to inform David that, unlike Saul, his son was to occupy his throne, and that the kingdom and the throne of his kingdom would be established forever. To David's son would God entrust the honor of building the temple. God said, *Thine house and thy kingdom shall be established forever before thee: thy throne shall be established forever* (II Samuel 7:16).

Spurgeon says, "How often God does for his servants what they desire to do for Him! David desired to build the Lord an house, and the Lord built him an house."

David's spirit is again revealed in his submission to God's plan for him. God allowed him to gather materials for his son to use.

God's servants do not take it ill that the Lord thwarts their plans and desires. A real servant learns what God's will is and yields his will to his Master's.

Under David's rule Israel reached its high-water mark. It has been called Israel's golden age. There were no shrines, no idol worship, no worldly functions when "the sweet singer of Israel," the "shepherd boy of Bethlehem," commanded the ship of state. His merchant caravans crossed the deserts and his routes went from the Nile to the Tigris and Euphrates, and Israel prospered.

When Israel was right with God, she was invincible against all odds.

DAVID'S FALL (II Samuel 11–20)

We wish the life of David could have ended before this chapter was written. The golden era had passed away and what was left was a checkered tale of sin and punishment. In all of God's Word there is no chapter more tragic or more full of warning for the child of God. It tells the story of David's fall. It is like an eclipse of the sun. His sins of adultery and virtual murder were a terrible blot on David's life. God forgave him, but the Word says, "The sword never departed from his house." He reaped just what he had sown. We see the harvest in his own house and in the nation.

Look over the steps in David's fall. You will find the steps downward in rapid succession.

First, he was idle. (II Sam. 11:1,2) It was the time for a king to go to war but he was not there. He remained in Jerusalem in the place of temptation. At evening-time he arose from off his bed and walked on the roof of his house. He was in that idle, listless mood which opens one to temptation. He saw the beautiful Bathsheba and he wanted her. His first sin was in the fact that "he saw." Don't look on evil. Ask God to keep your eyes. Refuse the admission of sin into your mind. If David had nipped the temptation in the bud, he would have saved himself a world of agony and awful sin. Instead of driving it out of his mind, he cherished it.

Next, "he sent and enquired." (II Sam. 11:3) He makes inquiry about this woman and then "he took." (v. 4) He brings her to his house. He forgets what is due to the faithful soldier whose wife she is.

But the next step is far more awful—his sin against Uriah, one of the bravest of his soldiers. He must get rid of him. He makes Joab the confidant in sin, his partner in murder.

This sin was the more terrible because it was committed by the head of the nation. This one had been notably favored by God. He was no longer a young man. He had passed through many experiences. Then, too, the excellent service of Uriah entitled him to rewards, not death.

Why do you suppose that this horrible story is given in the Bible? It bears the character of a beacon, warning the mariner against some of the most perilous rocks that are to be found in all the sea of life. Never neglect watching and praying. An hour's sleep left Samson at the mercy of Delilah. Don't fool with one sin, even in thought. The door may be opened to a dangerous brood. It doesn't take a whole box of matches to start a fire. One will do it!

A year later the prophet Nathan visited David and charged him with his sin. We can imagine the anguish of David's heart that year. We read of David's sincere repentance. (Psalm 51) God told David that his child should die because of his sin. See how David accepted this punishment. (II Sam. 12:13-32) When the child died, David worshiped God.

"A living sorrow is worse than a dead one," says a proverb. The death of his child was a grievous sorrow to David, but the living sorrow which he endured through his beloved son, Absalom, we cannot imagine. The rebellion of this young man is full of tragedy. Through a spy system he stole the kingdom from David.

Absalom was heartless and cruel. David suffered alike in the day of Absalom's victory and in the dark hour of his defeat and slaying. Read his lament over Absalom when he heard the news of his death. (II Sam. 18:19-33; 19:1-4)

DAVID'S LAST DAYS (II Samuel 20-24)

After the rebellion had been stopped, King David returned to his kingdom. New officers were installed and reconstruction began on every hand.

We see David's sin in numbering the people, because God had not told him to. The land was punished with a three day pestilence.

He gathered great provisions for the building of the temple and directed his son Solomon to build it. David was only seventy years old when he died.

This is the "man after God's heart." We need to understand David's life in order to understand and use the Psalms. We must know, too, why Christ was called the "Son of David." (Acts 13:22,23) David stands half way between Abraham and Christ.

David had his faults. He did much that was very

wrong, but he kept his nation from going into idolatry. Although his private sins were grievous, he stood like a rock for Jehovah. He sinned but he repented and gave God a chance to forgive and cleanse him. He illustrates the conflict that Paul describes in Romans 7. He was a great saint even though he was a great sinner.

The last verses of II Samuel 24:18-25 tell of King David's buying Araunah's threshing floor. He erected an altar there. This has special significance for it is on this site the great temple of Solomon was later built. On this sacred spot today stands the Mosque of Omar. It is a most galling thing to the Jews to have this sacred ground in the hands of the Moslem. The Jew cannot step his foot on the former temple area, the most hallowed spot in all the world to him.

THINK AND DO

Who was the popular king that followed Saul? Why was he popular?

Did God choose David because he was handsome like Saul?

How can we be guided by God?

What great prophecy did Nathan give to David?

Recall the steps in David's Fall.

God put David in public office. Can a Christian serve in political life today? What is our responsibility as Christian citizens?

Minimum Daily Requirements / Spiritual Vitamins

Sunday: DAVID MOURNS FOR JONATHAN AND SAUL
II Sam. 1:1-27

Monday: DAVID, KING OF JUDAH II Sam. 2:1-21; 3:1

Tuesday: DAVID, KING OF ALL ISRAEL II Sam. 5:1-25

Wednesday: DAVID'S HOUSE ESTABLISHED
II Sam. 7:1-29

Thursday: DAVID'S SIN II Sam. 11:1-27

Friday: DAVID'S REPENTANCE II Sam. 12:1-23;
Psalm 51

Saturday: DAVID NUMBERS THE PEOPLE
II Sam. 24:1-17

Chapter 11

LET'S LOOK AT KINGS and CHRONICLES

*KINGS AND CHRONICLES PORTRAY
JESUS CHRIST AS KING*

If we reject God, He will reject us. If we obey God, He will bless us. *In those days the LORD began to cut Israel short* (II Kings 10:32).

The original Hebrew in which I and II Kings were written, formed one book, and I and II Samuel another, and I and II Chronicles a third. When they were translated into the Greek language, they were divided by the translators because the Greek required one third more space than the Hebrew. Scrolls on which they were written were limited in length.

Probably the author of the Book of Kings was Jeremiah. The book was written while the first temple was standing. (I Kings 8:8)

THE SPLENDID REIGN OF SOLOMON (I Kings 1–10)

As the scene opens we find King David now old and stricken in years. He was prematurely aged for he was only seventy. His son Solomon was about nineteen. Because of David's feebleness we find a rebellion started against him. Adonijah's attempt to get his father's throne was natural because he was the oldest surviving son. (II Samuel 3:4) This rebellion called for prompt action which Nathan, the prophet, took. David saw that Solomon was the most fit to succeed him. Solomon was God's choice. (I Chronicles 22:9; I Kings 2:15) It was clear that the choice of Solomon was popular. (I Kings 1:39,40) Adonijah soon saw that opposition was useless. Because of this rebellion, Solomon was crowned before David's death. (I Kings 1:30,39,53)

Solomon received his religious training from Nathan the prophet. This wise prophet loved Solomon and gave him the name Jedidiah, "God's darling." (II Samuel 12:25) Solomon's reign began in a blaze of glory. It was splendor without surrender. And as with Saul, Solomon's life ended in an anti-climax.

His heart was not perfect with the LORD his God, as was the heart of David his father (I Kings 11:4). Remember, God wants our hearts!

Yet Solomon was a magnificient king; his throne was the grandest the world had ever seen and his life was filled with happenings of marvelous significance. His kingdom of 60,000 square miles was ten times as great as that which his father inherited. This shows what David accomplished during his reign.

After David's final words of admonition to his son to be absolutely loyal to Jehovah, he died, having reigned for forty years.

When the young Princess Victoria learned early one morning that she had become Queen of England, the first thing she did was to ask the Archbishop of Canterbury to pray for her. The Archbishop and Lord Chamberlain knelt down together and prayed that grace, strength and wisdom might be given to her throughout her reign. Are we to wonder why her reign was such a prosperous one? Governing is a serious business. Solomon realized its seriousness and began his reign with prayer.

God appeared to Solomon in a dream early in his reign and asked him to make a choice of anything that he might wish. The young king's choice revealed his feeling of inability to do all that was put upon him. What was his request of the Lord? God gave him the wisdom for which he asked. What is God's promise to us? (James 1:5)

The youth had not been swept off his feet by his father's praise when David twice called him a wise man. (I Kings 2:6-9) Solomon asked for a "hearing heart." Have we a heart that listens to the Spirit's voice?

Solomon was the wisest man the world ever saw until the coming of Him who could say of Himself, *a greater than Solomon is here* (Matthew 12:42).

All the earth acknowledged Solomon but when the greater than Solomon came His own received Him not. (John 1:11) That is tragedy. But have you received Him?

First Solomon organized his leaders. He gathered around him a wise company of officers of state, each

PALESTINE
TRIBES OF ISRAEL

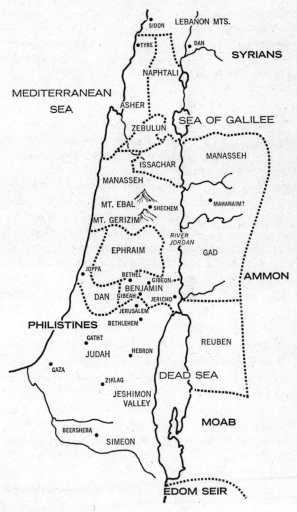

having his own department, for which he was responsible. This led to days of tremendous prosperity in the kingdom.

The greatest undertaking of Solomon's reign was the building of the temple. (I Kings 5:1–8:66) This was what his father David had longed to do. The immense foundation of great hewn stones upon which Solomon's temple was built remains till this day under the Mosque of Omar. One stone alone is thirty-eight feet, nine inches long. The huge stones, fragrant cedar wood and gold covering gave it unusual splendor.

The temple site was a historic spot. On Mount Moriah, Abraham offered up Isaac. (Genesis 22:2) We saw last week how David secured Araunah's threshing floor and here today the Mosque of Omar stands, the sacred spot of the Mohammedans. No Jew is allowed to step his foot upon this holy ground. So we see the Jews gathering from near and far to wail at the wall outside this area, to pray for mercy, and to ask God for deliverance from their enemy. The great stones which form this ancient wall were foundation stones of Solomon's temple.

Men used to have to make pilgrimages to the temple to meet God. Now we know a wonderful truth that our bodies are the temples of God. (I Cor. 3:16; 6:19)

Is your body a real temple? God wishes to live in you, but He cannot if you are defiled with sin.

Study each point in I Kings 9:1-28 and 10:14-29 to find the possible, not to say the probable, dangers to Solomon in all this wonderful glory. Note his high position, his great wisdom, his countless riches. It is hard not to forget God in the hour of such prosperity. One thinks only of his possessions. It was this very glory that led to Solomon's downfall.

Because of his backsliding, God raised up enemies to

vex Solomon. The Book of Ecclesiastes describes the futility of life to Solomon at this time.

The Queen of Sheba witnessed Solomon's reign at its zenith and saw the fulfillment of David's prayer for his son, offered about a year before David's death.

Solomon's reputation had probably spread through the voyages of his navy. (I Kings 9:21-28) Solomon's fame was associated with Jehovah. His fame concerning the name of the Lord was the thing that interested her Majesty, the Queen of Sheba. She was impressed (1) by Solomon himself, with his wisdom and wealth, I Kings 10:1,7; (2) his servants, verse 8; and (3) his God, verse 9.

THE KINGDOM TORN ASUNDER (I Kings 11–16)

Solomon reigned forty years, the second great period of the complete kingdom. (I Kings 11) At first all went well, but later there was serious trouble. Note that Saul, David and Solomon each reigned forty years, (Acts 13:21; II Sam. 5:4; I Kings 11:42)

Taxes under Solomon's reign had weighed the people down. Luxury and idolatry had broken down their morale. The kingdom now was to be divided.

A rise to such prosperity and power as Solomon enjoyed had its dangers. It cost money and meant increased taxation that grew into burdens that were unbearable and bred the seeds of unrest and revolution.

Solomon set up a great establishment in Jerusalem, built his famous temple, bringing in foreign workmen and materials to do it, and then he built himself a palace that dazzled his own subjects and his foreign visitors.

During this time there was corruption and graft, and under all these burdens the people grew restless and rebellious.

When Solomon's son, Rehoboam, threatened to levy

heavier burdens upon the people, his headstrong action added fuel to a fire which had been gathering and burning for nearly three hundred years, from the time of the judges.

The revolt of the ten tribes immediately followed (I Kings 12:16), though the two tribes of Judah and Benjamin remained loyal (I Kings 12:17). This tension led to the appointment of Jeroboam as king of the northern section. (v. 20)

A new name of great importance appeared in the pages of this story. Jeroboam was his name. He was a young man of low origin who had risen to recognition because of faithful service and deeds done. The prophet Ahijah made a startling revelation to Jeroboam. Using Oriental imagery, he took off his new coat *and he said to Jeroboam. Take thee ten pieces: for thus saith the LORD, the God of Israel, Behold, I will rend the kingdom out of the hand of Solomon, and will give ten tribes to thee* (I Kings 11:31).

The kingdom was divided. The judgment was upon Solomon for his long years of luxury and pride and power. Every ruler should look ahead and see toward what rocks he may be driving his kingdom, and whether or not he is heading toward the day when his power shall be rent out of his hand.

Have we not seen in our day men, rising to great wealth and power in which they have piled up millions, stripped to nothing and fleeing from justice?

Things do not happen by accident. There is a cause at the root of every revolution. The event may come as suddenly as an explosion, or as the eruption of a volcano, but somewhere secret causes are at work undermining the structure. The French Revolution had its roots down under centuries of oppression.

Religious apostasy had been gnawing like a deadly

worm at the root of Israel's life. One day the tree fell. Nothing destroys a nation's life like religious decline.

Take the sun out of the sky and there will be no grass, or flowers, or orchards. Take God out of our sky and there will be no homes, or schools, or social life.

Do you think that religious decline had anything to do with causing World War I or II?

Do you think it would be possible for our own country to ever become divided?

Though they didn't know it, the people were carrying out the divine purpose. (I Kings 12:15; 11:29-33) God could not overlook the disobedience of Solomon in His clearest commands.

The kingdom of God's chosen people was divided. It has been divided for almost 3,000 years. It was divided through sin. We see this kingdom go to pieces and finally into captivity. (II Kings 17,25)

It is part of the gospel, the "good news," that those two great sections of divided Israel are going to be united again on this earth at Christ's return in glory. Read the wonderful passages in Isaiah 11:10-13; Ezekiel 37:15-28.

THE MINISTRY OF ELIJAH
(I Kings 17–22; II Kings 1:1–2:2)

Elijah was a bolt of fire that God let loose upon wicked Ahab and idolatrous Israel. He flashed across the page of history as sudden and terrible as a flash of lightning. *Elijah the Tishbite, who was of the inhabitants of Gilead* is his brief biography by which he was introduced. His name Elijah means "Jehovah is my God." It fitted him perfectly. He was the most outstanding of the prophets. Follow his sudden appearance, his undaunted courage, his zeal, the heights of his triumphs on Mount Carmel, the depths of his despondence, the glorious rapture into heaven in the whirlwind, his reappearance on the Mount of Transfiguration.

He was a striking character from the highlands of Gilead. His long thick hair hung over a cloak of sheepskin. Jehovah sent him to do away with the awful worship of Baal during the reign of Ahab who had married the wicked heathen princess, Jezebel. Suddenly emerging from the desert and standing before the corrupt king in the splendor of his court, the stern prophet boldly said, *As the LORD God of Israel liveth, before whom I stand, there shall not be dew nor rain these years, but according to my word* (I Kings 17:1). He was given power to shut up the heavens so they would not rain for three and a half years. He called down fire from heaven before the prophets of Baal at Mount Carmel. He was the evangelist of his day, thundering out warnings to this idolatrous people. The events in this great career will intrigue you. Read them.

THE MINISTRY OF ELISHA (II Kings 1–9)

Elisha succeeded Elijah. He was beneficent in contrast to the fiery Elijah.

Elijah trained Elisha as his successor. Elisha's ministry lasted fifty years. Most of his miracles were deeds of kindness and mercy. Elisha had a great influence upon the kings of the day and although he did not approve of what they did, he was always coming to their rescue.

Elijah and Elisha are in marked contrast to one another:

Elijah, the prophet of judgment, law, severity.

Elisha, the prophet of grace, love, tenderness.

Baal worship was introduced by the wicked Jezebel and after thirty years was exterminated by Elijah, Elisha and Jehu.

The Corruption Of Israel

Jeroboam, the king of the Northern Kingdom, Israel, made Shechem his capital. It seemed the natural place because it was in the center of the land.

It was the custom, according to the law, to go up to Jerusalem regularly to worship. (Deut. 12:11,14; 16:6, 15,16; I Sam. 1:3,7) Jeroboam was afraid to have his ten tribes journey to Jerusalem, the capital of Rehoboam's kingdom, to worship God. He made two golden calves and placed them in convenient spots—Bethel (Gen. 28:11-19) in the south, and Dan (Judges 18:29, 30) in the north of the kingdom so the people would not have to go to Jerusalem.

Over twenty times he is described as *Jeroboam the son of Nebat, who made Israel to sin.* Beware of manmade religion. We must worship where and how God tells us!

God says, *Not forsaking the assembling of ourselves together, as the manner of some is* (Hebrews 10:25). God knows we need fellowship in worship to keep the spiritual coals alive, but we hear people say constantly that they can worship better alone in the woods or by the sea. Learn not to do what God asks you to do. Remember a request from a king is a command!

After 256 years the people were carried into captivity by the king of Assyria. (II Kings 17) Many of God's prophets had warned Israel of captivity but they would not turn from their idolatry to Jehovah.

The Assyrians were great and cruel warriors. They built their kingdom on their pillage from other countries. Their practices were horrible. They skinned men alive, cut out their tongues, put out their eyes, dismembered their bodies and then made mounds of the skulls of men to instill fear! For three hundred years Assyria was a world empire.

THE CAPTIVITY OF JUDAH (II Kings 13–25)

The Southern Kingdom tried to conquer the Northern Kingdom. For eighty years there was continuous war between them. But they failed. Then there was a period of eighty years of peace between these two kingdoms following the marriage of the son of Jehoshaphat (southern king) to the daughter of Ahab (northern king). Finally there was a period of fifty years when they intermittently warred with one another until the captivity.

In the Southern Kingdom there was only one dynasty (Davidic) from King Rehoboam to Zedekiah. The great prophets of that day were Isaiah, Nathan, Jeremiah, Joel and Zephaniah.

About 136 years after the Northern Kingdom had been taken into captivity by Assyria, the Southern Kingdom was taken captive by Nebuchadnezzar, king of Babylon. Jerusalem was destroyed, the temple burned and the princes led away. The people had forgotten God and refused to listen to the warnings of the prophets.

God wanted His people to learn the lesson of obedience and dependence upon Him.

In I Kings we see the kingdom of Israel, filled with pride and arrogance, falling apart. In II Kings, sinning yet more, Israel goes into captivity. Surely the way of the transgressor is hard. The history of the Jews is a record of God's dealings with disobedient children. In all His punishment, He is kind and merciful for He loves them still.

The secret of the downfall of the Jewish people is found in II Kings 3:2. *And he wrought evil in the sight of the LORD.* Be loyal and true to God. It does not pay to do evil.

As we look at the roster of the kings, we see a poor, pitiful, dwindling procession:

In Israel from Jeroboam to Hoshea. Then captivity for the ten tribes (about 721 B.C.).

In Judah, from Rehoboam to Zedekiah. Then the burden and discipline of the brick-kiln for Judah (586 B.C.).

The moving figures and powerful factors of those days were the prophets Elijah and Elisha.

Elijah stalked forth abruptly like the heroes of the old French romance, out of a hole in the wall. Read I Kings 17:1 where Elijah said, *As the LORD God of Israel liveth, before whom I stand.* And there he stood for God, like a rock, in face of all the weakness of Israel.

We ask today, *Where is the LORD God of Elijah* (II Kings 2:14)? Would that we might see some of this old-time power.

Elijah was the champion of the Most High. He brought God to the people. He was the pastor-evangelist of Israel's day.

THE BOOK OF I CHRONICLES

1. The long dry lists of names which are contained in these books have a purpose. They connect David, the forerunner and type of Christ, with the historic figures of Israel. The record of the great families of the nation are here. See what a great spiritual lesson one can get right in the midst of these lists, as in I Chronicles 5:20.

2. This book is David's book. Thrilling accounts of the heroic deeds of the national hero, David, and the deeds of his mighty men occur here. See especially chapter 11.

3. One may get great inspirational and spiritual lessons from I Chronicles. See especially the beautiful psalm of thanksgiving in 16:7-36, and the challenge of I Chronicles 29:5.

THE BOOK OF II CHRONICLES

We may divide II Chronicles into two divisions:

1. Solomon and the period of Israel's magnificence: (Chapters 1–9) Aside from what we already know of Solomon, II Chronicles tells us a great deal more, especially about his temple and his great rule. See chapters seven and eight. Read II Chronicles 7:14 for another great spiritual lesson.

2. The kings from the death of Solomon to the time of the captivities: Remember the names of Jehoshaphat (chapters 17–20), Joash (23; 24), Uzziah (26 and Isaiah 6), and Hezekiah (29–32). What spiritual lessons do you get from the lives of these rulers?

THINK AND DO

What great request did Solomon make of God when he was still a youth?

Solomon was a great builder. He built five palace buildings, a city (Megiddo), stables for his horses, a fleet of ships, plants for refining ore, etc., but what was Solomon's greatest building project? (I Kings 6:1–7:51; 9:15,26)

What tragic mistakes did Solomon make?

Does success often turn men's heads?

The Kingdoms of Israel and Judah were founded on their belief in one God and their worship of Him. Compare with the foundations of America. Are our leaders, like Solomon, ignoring foundations today?

What men did God send to warn His people of their sins? They were called prophets.

Was Israel's downfall caused from enemies without or "fifth columns" of godlessness and greed and sin within?

What are some of the things that are undermining Christian America today? Add any more that you know of to this list: drinking, divorce, race prejudice, un-Christian homes, no God in education, godless men in government, etc.

Tell of the captivity and decline of the Kingdoms of Israel and Judah.

Minimum Daily Requirements / Spiritual Vitamins

Sunday: BUILDING AND DEDICATING THE TEMPLE I Kings 6:1-14; 8:22-53

Monday: SOLOMON'S GLORIOUS REIGN I Kings 10:1-29

Tuesday: THE KINGDOM DIVIDED I Kings 12:1-33

Wednesday: THE PROPHET ELIJAH I Kings 17:1–18:46

Thursday: ELIJAH AND ELISHA II Kings 2:1-22

Friday: THE CAPTIVITY OF ISRAEL (THE NORTHERN KINGDOM) II Kings 17:7-23

Saturday: THE CAPTIVITY OF JUDAH (THE SOUTHERN KINGDOM) II Kings 25:1-21

Chapter 12

LET'S LOOK AT EZRA and NEHEMIAH

EZRA AND NEHEMIAH PORTRAY
JESUS CHRIST, OUR RESTORER

Again we find that Ezra and Nehemiah were one book in the Hebrew Bible as were the two books of Samuel and Kings. These books tell the story of the return of God's chosen people after the exile. It gives the record of one of the most important events in Jewish history—the return from exile in Babylon.

"Remember Thy word to Moses," prayed Nehemiah. (Neh. 1:8) The Books of Ezra and Nehemiah tell the story of how God remembered and how He brought back His people from the exiles. Jeremiah 29:10-13 tells us of this remembrance.

During the captivity, the prophets, Jeremiah and Ezekiel, told the Jews of their restoration and predicted that they would return to their own land and rebuild Jerusalem. Jeremiah, the prophet, told them this would happen at the end of seventy years. *For thus saith the LORD, That after seventy years be accomplished at Babylon I will visit you, and perform my good word toward you, in causing you to return to this place* (Jeremiah 29:10).

You remember that the Books of Kings ended with the story of the captivity of first the Northern Kingdom of Israel and then the Southern Kingdom of Judah.

Daniel was carried away captive to Babylon at the time of the captivity. The last incident in the history was the story of Daniel in the lions' den. (Daniel 6:16-24) This happened about ten years before Cyrus became king over Babylon. Daniel was an old man now when these present events took place.

The Book of Ezra Looks Backward and Forward

LOOKING BACKWARD—We find a second exodus for captive Israel. The first exodus was out of Egypt. This second exodus was from Babylon. This time Ezra is the leader in the place of Moses. He, like Moses, is an inspired writer and leader. Both men were great organizers, law-givers, and teachers raised up to fulfill God's gracious purpose and bring captive Israel out of bondage. Both of these great leaders dealt with Israel in a merciful and strong way.

LOOKING AHEAD—In history it is like the landing of our Pilgrim Fathers on a bleak and hostile shore. They came in timid, struggling relays back to Jerusalem. But God gave them a foothold. It was His city and it is His city still. He will again bring back His own; He will raise up Zion out of ruins.

The rebuilding of the national life of the Jews covered one hundred years.

There are two periods of time that are very important.

1. Twenty years (537-517 B.C.) from the first year of Cyrus to the sixth year of Darius when the people under Zerubbabel, the governor, and Joshua, the priest, rebuilt the temple. For this period read Ezra 1-6; Zechariah and Haggai; the first chapters of I Chronicles; the last two verses of II Chronicles; Psalms 126; 137; and the reference to Cyrus in Isaiah 44:23 to 45:8.

2. Twenty-five years (458-433 B.C.) when Nehemiah, the governor, and Ezra, the priest, rebuilt the wall of Jerusalem and restored the city. Malachi was the prophet of this day.

Ezra gives the record of both of these periods.

Nehemiah tells of the second period, the building of the walls.

The Jews were taken captive first by Assyria (II Kings 17), then by Babylon. (II Kings 25) They were restored to their own land under the Persian Empire. The Babylonians had been conquered by the Medes and Persians. The ten northern tribes who were carried away to Assyria never returned. What has become of them is of great interest.

LOOK AT THE WORLD

During This Time

GREECE—Days of Socrates and Pericles. Athens at the peak of her glory.

INDIA—Buddha—557-447 B.C.

CHINA—Confucius—551-478 B.C.

In 537 B.C. The first Jews return to Jerusalem from Babylon.

In 516 B.C. Temple restored.

In 479 B.C. Esther becomes queen of Persia. (She is wife of Xerxes.)

In 458 B.C. Ezra leads second expedition from Babylon.

In 445 B.C. Nehemiah builds wall of Jerusalem.

RETURN UNDER ZERUBBABEL AND REBUILDING THE TEMPLE (Ezra 1–6)

As the scene opens (Ezra 1:1-6), we find Cyrus, king of Persia, making a proclamation throughout his kingdom permitting the Jews who were captives in his kingdom to return to Jerusalem.

Two hundred years before, God has prophesied that He would do this. He named Cyrus as the one He would use. The record of this remarkable prophecy, which calls a king by his name two hundred years before he was born, is found in Isaiah 44:28; 45:1-4. No doubt this proclamation of Cyrus was due in part to the fact that he saw these words of Isaiah.

Daniel's influence in the court was very powerful. He had been the Disraeli of the court in Babylon. He was one of the princes carried away by Nebuchadnezzar to his court. Now he was an old man.

At Cyrus' first call (537 B.C.) (Ezra 1:1-4), no more than 50,000 Jews availed themselves of the opportunity of returning to Jerusalem under Zerubbabel. Notice from this time the Israelites are called Jews because most of them were of the tribe of Judah and the name Jews comes from Judah.

Cyrus gave back to Zerubbabel the gold vessels which Nebuchadnezzar had taken from the temple in Jerusalem. (Ezra 1:5-11) They started back over seven hundred miles of trackless desert from Babylon to Jerusalem.

At the time of the captivity, seventy years before, only the better classes were taken into Babylon. The rest were left in their own land to suffer. (Jeremiah 24:5-8; 44:15) Everyone did not return; only the earnest and pious Jews went back. It was a time of real sifting among the people. Most of them after seventy years had built homes and established themselves and were only too content to remain in Babylon. They did not care to face the dangers and hardships of returning across the desert and arriving in a city that had been destroyed.

Although the leaders were from the tribe of Judah, no doubt there were representatives from the whole of Israel. Only those who loved God were ready to make the attempt. Many of the Jews had been born in Babylon during the seventy years. These were not considered captives, but exiles.

Everything is taken care of when God is in charge. Not only money for rebuilding the temple in Jerusalem, but traveling expenses and all other needs were provided by God at Cyrus' direction. (Ezra 1:4,6) Someone has said that God used Babylon as the safety deposit vault for the silver and gold vessels of the temple.

The names of those who returned are given in chapter two. They laid the foundation of the temple the first thing upon returning. It was a time of great rejoicing. It is interesting to notice that before they built homes for themselves, they first thought of a house for the Lord. They did not build the temple first but the altar. (Ezra 3:2)

The place where sin must be dealt with must come first in every life. The heart must be right if God is to bless. The altar was the center of the Jew's religion, the cross the center of the Christian faith.

Read about the hindrances to the work. (Ezra 4:1-22) Hindrances to all real work for God are to be expected. The church must not have the help of the world.

The opposition disheartened them. They needed Haggai's message. Refer to the Book of Haggai.

Haggai and Zechariah, the prophets, encouraged the people from within the ranks (Ezra 4:23–5:17), and within four years the temple was complete and dedicated. (Ezra 6)

Zerubbabel's temple was very plain and simple. It was not the sumptuous edifice that Solomon's was. In fact, it was in such contrast to the elegance of the first temple that the old men who had seen Solomon's temple wept aloud. But it was God's house and so the people thanked God and took courage.

RETURN AND REFORMATION UNDER EZRA
(Ezra 7–10)

It is not until the seventh chapter that Ezra appears in person (458 B.C.). At least sixty years after the Jews had first returned to Jerusalem, he led a second expedition from Babylon to reinforce the struggling colonists in Palestine. Ezra bore a commission from Artaxerxes, the king (Ezra 7:11–8:14), who half blindly aided in accomplishing God's plans for His people. Read Ezra 7:25 and find how impressed the king was with Ezra's love of God's Word. Oh, that we might live in such a way that others would learn to have respect for God's Book!

This contingent, under Ezra, consisted of about 1700 Jews. It took them about four months to make the journey, and it was financed by King Artaxerxes. (Ezra 7:12-26) It was thirteen years later that this same king authorized Nehemiah to build the walls of Jerusalem.

(Nehemiah 2) Cyrus, Darius and Artaxerxes, the three Persian kings, were very friendly to the Jews.

Ezra was the Thomas Jefferson of his time, laying the constitutional foundations for the future. To him, we are indebted for codifying Israel's laws and the formation of her scripture canon.

When Ezra returned to Jerusalem, he found things even worse than he had expected. Although the people had not returned to idolatry, they had intermarried with the people of the land and had done everything that the heathen had done. (Ezra 9:1-4) The princes and rulers were the worst offenders. Ezra rent his garments and literally pulled out his hair in grief! Read Ezra's touching prayer and confession. (9:5-15)

As Ezra was praying and weeping before God, a great congregation assembled. What happened? (Read Ezra 10:1-44.) The people who had gathered about him through the long hours of the day came to a consciousness of the greatness of their sin as they saw how it affected Ezra. Finally one of their number spoke and acknowledged the sin. At once Ezra led them into a sacred covenant with God. Read what God says about confession of sin. (I John 1:9)

If you turn now to Nehemiah 9, you will find the prayer of Nehemiah. It never pays to pass over the prayers of the Bible. Prayer is the most important privilege of a Christian. Nehemiah's prayer began where Ezra's ended—with utter surrender to God. (Compare Neh. 9:1, 2 with Ezra 9:15-10.)

God had definitely promised to bring the Jews back after seventy years in Babylon. (Jer. 25:11,12; 29:10) We read in the very first verse of Ezra that it was to fulfill this word that *the LORD stirred up the spirit of Cyrus* to proclaim the restoration. (Look this up!) But it is through prayer that God wishes to have His will brought to pass. The restoration was wholly undeserved by Israel but purposed in "God's heart of mercy."

THE BOOK OF NEHEMIAH

REPAIRING THE CITY WALLS (Nehemiah 1–7)

Nehemiah was the cupbearer at the court of King Artaxerxes. This was a position of high honor. But in this position of familiarity with the king, he had not forgotten his people. The news that was brought to him about Jerusalem made him very sad. This sadness could not be wholly hidden and the king detected it. The Jews had been back home for one hundred years, but had made no attempt to build Jerusalem beyond the restoration of the temple because their enemies made it almost impossible.

Artaxerxes' stepmother was Esther, the Jewess, who no doubt was still alive. It may have been that Nehemiah received his appointment through her influence. He was loyal enough to his people to leave the luxury of a king's court and go back to rebuild Jerusalem, the capital of his homeland. The king gave consent. We find, even today, Jews everywhere long to see Jerusalem flourish and turn their faces there as their homeland. An example of this interest is seen in the Zionist movement.

When Nehemiah reached Jerusalem in 445 B.C., Ezra had been there for thirteen years. Ezra was a priest and had been teaching the people the Word of God. But Nehemiah was a civil governor. He had come with the authority of the king of Persia to build the walls of Jerusalem. After he had been there only three days, he went up and viewed the walls at night. When he saw their dilapidated condition, he encouraged the people to begin building immediately. This was accomplished in fifty-two days by assigning the work to each family. Their attitude was expressed in the sentence, *the people had a mind to work* (Nehemiah 4:6). Nehemiah was a real engineer.

First the Samaritans, the enemies of the Jews, derided them. They hindered their work so that the Jews had to keep watch night and day. The derision was turned to anger and Nehemiah divided the men into two groups, one keeping watch while the other worked.

Then opposition rose within the ranks. Some of the Jews became tired and complained that there was so much rubbish that the walls could not be built. Remember, all this had to be removed in a thick canvas pad on the carrier's back; there were no wheelbarrows or cars to convey the material.

Then, they complained that the rich were demanding usury that they were unable to pay.

Again the enemies tried by craft to bring Nehemiah away from his building, but Nehemiah only prayed and again he foiled his enemy.

The Persian kings were ever the friends of the Jews.

Nehemiah gave the city of Jerusalem into the charge of his brother Hanani. (Nehemiah 7:1-4) Then he took a census. (7:5-73) The whole number was 42,360 besides 7,337 servants and 245 singing men and women.

All the people gathered together in the street before the water-gate in the city of Jerusalem and requested Ezra, the scribe, to bring out the book of the Law of Moses. He stood upon a pulpit of wood and read and explained the Law to the people. (Nehemiah 8:1-13) This public reading brought true repentance to the people and a great revival broke out. When Josiah found the book of the Law, a great reformation started. When Martin Luther read the Bible, the Protestant

Reformation began. We need to have the Word read today!

Their captivity in Babylon cured the Jews of idolatry. You remember up to that time in spite of all the warnings of the prophets, the people would worship the idols of the peoples around them. But from the days of captivity to the present, about 2500 years, the Jews have never been guilty of this sin. The Jews had intermarried with these idolatrous neighbors and this was the reason for their sin. Intermarriage of Christians with those who do not believe is a dangerous thing today. Paul says, *Be ye not unequally yoked together with unbelievers* (II Corinthians 6:14).

Remember, Nehemiah left a life of ease, luxury and security for a life of toil, danger and heartbreaks. He was a reformer! And no one appreciates the man who tries to reform him.

Nehemiah was a man of prayer. We do not find a blot on his character. He was fearless and courageous.

THE BOOK OF NEHEMIAH MAY BE DIVIDED:

1. **REPAIRING THE CITY'S WALLS**...Nehemiah 1–7
2. **REPAIRING THE PEOPLE'S MORALS** ....Nehemiah 8–13

THINK AND DO

Describe the Nation's Homecoming. What names are important? What was the first thing to be rebuilt when the Jews returned to their homeland?

What were the hindrances to the work?

What are hindrances to the work of the church today?

What great contribution did Ezra make?

What contribution did Nehemiah make?

Nehemiah was a statesman. Do we need Christian statesmen today? Can a man be a true patriot and a Christian today?

What was one of the greatest social sins of the Jews? Is this one of the sins of our day?

What moral conditions should be remedied today? What do young people think of smoking? social drinking? swearing? petting? gambling? cheating? stealing?

Minimum Daily Requirements / Spiritual Vitamins

Sunday: JEWS RETURN TO JERUSALEM Ezra 1–3
Monday: DISCOURAGEMENT AND JOY Ezra 4–6
Tuesday: EZRA'S EXPEDITION Ezra 7–10
Wednesday: NEHEMIAH REBUILDS THE WALL Neh. 1–3
Thursday: OVERCOMING OPPOSITION Neh. 4–6
Friday: NEHEMIAH REBUILDS THE MORALS Neh. 7–9
Saturday: REFORMING THROUGH RELIGION Neh. 11–13

Chapter 13

A QUICK LOOK
AT THE OLD TESTAMENT

GENESIS THROUGH NEHEMIAH

OUTLINE OF OLD TESTAMENT HISTORY

I. **PERIOD OF PATRIARCHS:**
Adam to Moses...........................Genesis

II. **PERIOD OF GREAT LEADERS:**
Moses to Saul...................Exodus–I Samuel

III. **PERIOD OF GREAT KINGS:**
Saul to the Babylonian
captivity..Samuel, Kings, Chronicles, prophetical books

IV. **PERIOD OF FOREIGN KINGS:**
Captivity to coming of
Christ.......Ezra, Nehemiah, Esther, Daniel, Ezekiel

I. **PERIOD OF PATRIARCHS: ADAM TO MOSES**
Bible account found in Book of Genesis.
We find in this period:
1. God's chosen men
2. God's chosen family
3. God's chosen people—the tribes of Israel

1. God's Chosen Men

In the beginning we find no nations. God chose men who made Him known, but the earth became more and more wicked. (Genesis 6:5)

The chosen men were:
Adam, created in God's image
Seth, his godly son
Enoch, who walked with God
Noah, who built the ark
Shem, (Noah's son) and his descendants
The important events during this time were:

Creation ....(Genesis 1; 2)
Fall ....(Genesis 3)
Flood ....(Genesis 6–8)
Babel and the dispersion.............(Genesis 11)

Four great nations were established as a result:

Egypt in North Africa

Phoenicia on the Mediterranean

Chaldea between the Tigris and Euphrates rivers

Assyria, north of Chaldea

2. God's Chosen Family

The race had failed (Genesis 6:5); now God limited His promises to a single family. He calls Abraham to become the father of this nation.

The important events are:

Abraham called

(Genesis 12:1–25:11)

Jacob chosen

(Genesis 25:19–36:43)

Joseph cherished

(Genesis 45; 46)

3. God's Chosen People

Twelve tribes become a nation.

II. PERIOD OF GREAT LEADERS: MOSES TO SAUL

Bible account given in Exodus to I Samuel.

We find in this period:

1. The Exodus—Exodus
2. The wilderness wandering—Exodus, Leviticus, Numbers, Deuteronomy
3. Conquest of Canaan—Joshua
4. The rule of the judges—Judges

III. PERIOD OF KINGS: SAUL TO THE BABYLONIAN CAPTIVITY

Bible account given in Samuel, Kings, Chronicles and the Prophets. Tribal life developed into national life.

We find in this period:

1. The united kingdom—Saul, David, Solomon

2. The divided kingdom—Kings of Israel—Northern Kingdom

Kings of Judah—Southern Kingdom

The fall of the Northern Kingdom

The fall of the Southern Kingdom

IV. PERIOD OF FOREIGN KINGS: CAPTIVITY TO CHRIST

Bible account in Ezra, Nehemiah, Esther, Daniel and Ezekiel. God was preparing the land, the people and the world for the coming Christ.

We find in this period:

Restoration under Persian kings.

TELL THE CONSECUTIVE STORY OF THE OLD TESTAMENT BY FOLLOWING THESE WORDS:

EVENTS	Noah
Creation	Shem, Ham and Japheth
Fall and promise	Abraham
Flood	Jacob
Dispersion	Joseph
Call of Abraham	Moses
Bondage in Egypt	Joshua
Exodus	Judges
Wilderness wanderings	Eli
Entering the promised land	Samuel
Rule of the judges	Saul
The united kingdom	David
The divided kingdom	Solomon
The captivities	Southern kings
The return to Jerusalem	Northern kings
PERSONS	Foreign kings—
Adam	Nebuchadnezzar
Eve	Ezra
Cain and Abel	Nehemiah
Enoch	

"THIS MAN" QUIZ

WHO ARE THE FOLLOWING?

1. This Man (a) was never born; (b) never had a birthday; (c) owned a great estate; (d) was perfect physically; (e) was a great zoologist, gave every animal a name.

(Adam)

2. This Man (a) was father of the oldest man in the world; (b) lived a godly life in one of the wickedest generations in the world; (c) was the only man in 3,000 years who did not die; (d) walked into heaven.

(Enoch)

3. This Man (a) was a great evangelist—preached one hundred years without a convert, but he saved his family of seven by his faith in God; (b) was a great ship builder, but built a huge ship on a desert, miles from the sea; (c) never had to launch his ship into the sea—the sea came to it and lifted it to the top of a mountain; (d) gathered the greatest collection of animals the world has ever known; (e) had sons who were the fathers of the nations of the world.

(Noah)

4. This Man was akin to a covered wagon pioneer: (a) he left a great city of culture at God's request and travelled across a trackless desert; (b) he left a beautiful home and lived in a tent for one hundred years; (c) he was called "a friend of God"; (d) he was the father of a great nation; (e) his son was born after he was one hundred years old; (f) angels visited him.

(Abraham)

5. This Man (a) and his young friend believed God when no one else would; (b) was a great general; (c) did not have to build a bridge to transport his army into the land that he wanted to conquer; (d) used trumpets instead of bombers and priests instead of trained soldiers to destroy a city.

(Joshua)

6. This Man (a) was an adopted child; (b) lived amidst the wealth of the day; (c) enjoyed unlimited education; (d) in spite of this, chose to identify himself with the poor people from whom he came rather than with the rulers with whom he lived; (e) was forced to live in a desert for forty years; (f) was chosen as the leader of about 3,000,000 people and led them out from under the bondage of the strongest ruler of his day without firing a shot; (g) made slaves become rich overnight; (h) was the meekest man on earth and yet he lost his temper; (i) talked with God; (j) died an unknown death; (k) was buried by no man.

(Moses)

Chapter 14

LET'S LOOK AT ESTHER

ESTHER PORTRAYS JESUS CHRIST,
OUR ADVOCATE

REJECTION OF VASHTI (Read Esther 1)

As this book opens King Ahasuerus was entertaining the nobles and princes of his kingdom in the royal palace at Shushan. The banquet was on a colossal scale. It lasted 180 days. (Esther 1:4) Think of a celebration for six months! The men were feasting in the gorgeous palace gardens and the women were entertained by the beautiful Queen Vashti in her private apartment.

Shushan was the winter residence of the Persian

kings. Remember Nehemiah was in the palace in Shushan. (Neh. 1:1)

When the king and princes were in the midst of their drunken revelry, the king called for Vashti, so that he could show off her beauty. Of course, no Persian woman would do this. It was an outrage to her womanhood. Drunkenness had disregarded the most sacred rules of Oriental etiquette. The seclusion of the harem was to be violated for the amusement of the dissolute king and his boon companions. Vashti refused. This made the king a laughing stock. To defend himself, he deposed the queen. (Esther 1:12-22)

Remember, modesty is the crown jewel of womanhood. Never be false to your pure ideals.

Remember you are bound to protect this crown jewel in womanhood.

CROWNING OF ESTHER (Read Esther 2)

The minute Ahasuerus saw Esther, he made her his queen. The little Jewish orphan girl, brought up by her cousin Mordecai, was lifted to the Persian throne which at this time comprised over half the then known world.

Two years after Xerxes (Ahasuerus) fought the famous battles of Thermopylae and Salamis he married Esther. She was his queen for thirteen years. Esther, no doubt, lived for many years into the reign of her stepson, Artaxerxes. Under this king, Nehemiah rebuilt Jerusalem. It was Esther's marriage to this famous Persian monarch that gave the Jews enough prestige at this court and made it possible for Nehemiah to rebuild Jerusalem. (See Neh. 2:1-8.)

To make the story of this Jewish girl more real and interesting, let us give you a little description of the palace. The foundation was a platform fifty feet high, and covered an area of two and a half acres. Underneath was a vast sewer system, miles in length, through

137

which one may walk today. The walls of the palace were covered with the most magnificent carvings, reliefs, and sculptures. Two large rooms in the Louvre display these treasures. When the rubbish was finally cleared away during the excavation, they found these carvings preserved, as fresh and beautiful as when Queen Esther walked through the corridors.

The second chapter describes the scene in this palace. Richly colored awnings were stretched across from marble pillars to silver rods, shading the exalted guests as they reclined on gold and silver seats while they feasted gluttonously and drank heavily, day after day. (Esther 1:5-8)

There was a grand audience hall where men came from the four corners of the earth to pay their honor to the great king, Esther's husband. The giant columns still rise in their grandeur, speaking of the former glory of the palace. This was the palace to which Esther was brought as queen.

Here, parenthetically, occurs the story of Mordecai's saving the king's life. This account figures prominently later in the book. (Esther 2:21-23)

PLOTTING OF HAMAN (Read Esther 3; 4)

We see a form casting a shadow across the picture. This scene is one of sorrow and mourning.

In Esther 3–5 we read of the ascendancy of a man by the name of Haman, an Amalekite.

Haman was the Judas of Israel. He was a wicked monster in the life of God's chosen people. Today during the reading of the Book of Esther in a Jewish synagogue, at the feast of Purim, the congregation may be found taking part in a chorus at every mention of the name Haman. "May his name be blotted out," while boys pound stones and bits of wood on which his hated name is written.

138

When Haman appears in the Book of Esther, he had just been exalted to the highest position under the king of Persia. (Esther 3:1) The high honor turned his head. He swelled with vanity and was bitterly humiliated when a porter at the gate did not do homage to him. (Esther 3:2) Mordecai would worship Jehovah only. He would not bow before men.

Inflated with pride, Haman could not endure the indifference of even his lowliest subject. The slight of Mordecai was magnified into a capital offense. Mordecai, a Jew, could not give divine honor to a man! Haman became so enraged that he wanted to have a wholesale massacre of all the Jews in the kingdom. (Esther 3:6) To determine the day his enemies should be destroyed, he cast lots which fell on the thirteenth day of March, just ten months away. (Esther 3:7) Haman tried to prove to the king that all the Jews were disloyal subjects. He offered to pay the king a $19,400,000 bribe to sign a royal decree that meant that every man, woman, and child who was a Jew should be killed and all their property be taken. (Esther 3:9)

You can imagine the fasting and praying and the weeping in sackcloth among the Jews! (Esther 4:1-3)

Queen Esther saw it all and inquired of Mordecai what it meant. He gave her a copy of the king's decree which told the sad story. Then he added, *And who knoweth whether thou art come to the kingdom for such a time as this* (Esther 4:14)?

It would be well for each one of us to pause and ask himself this same question. Why has God allowed me to live at this particular hour? To do what is right may mean that we must jeopardize our lives. Then we must face the issue and answer with this young queen, *And if I perish, I perish.*

139

VENTURE OF ESTHER (Read Esther 5)

Queen Esther answers the challenge of Mordecai. She, who had been placed in the palace on flowery beds of ease, had not succumbed to the luxury of her surroundings. She chose a course at terrible danger to herself for the sake of her oppressed people, the Jews.

There is one thing to do always. Do what is right and leave the rest to God. God prepares men for emergencies. Failure is not sin; faithlessness is.

There is a time to act. There is a tide in the affairs of men which, taken at the flood, leads on to fortune. Act when God speaks. Great illustrations may be found in both Scripture and secular history of those who dared to obey God.

The beauty of Esther is that she is not spoiled by her great elevation. Though she has become the queen of a great king, she does not forget the kind porter who brought her up from childhood. When she once accepted her dreaded task, she proceeded to carry it out with courage. It was a daring act for her to enter into the presence of the king unsummoned. Who could tell what this fickle monarch would do? Think what he had done to Vashti!

When she had been received by the king, she used her resources. She knew the king's weakness for good living, so she invited him to a banquet. Read what happened that night when the king could not sleep. (See Esther 6:1-11.) How was Haman trapped? (Esther 6:6) At the second banquet Esther pleaded for her own life. She had Haman on the spot.

The king granted Esther's wish. Haman was hung on the very scaffold which he had prepared for Mordecai, and Mordecai was elevated to the place of honor next to the king.

Haman had planned well but he had left God out. As

you study God's Word, you will find that through the ages Satan has ever tried to destroy God's people, the Church, yes, and Christ, without reckoning on God. But God has thwarted his plans. Even the *gates of hell shall not prevail against* His Church.

DELIVERANCE OF THE JEWS (Read Esther 6–10)

The Book of Esther closes with the account of the establishment of the Feast of Purim and the lifting of Mordecai to the place made vacant by Haman. (Esther 10:3) The Jewish porter became the grand vizier of Persia. The Feast of Purim was to be celebrated annually. It is always inspired by the dramatic story of Esther.

The Feast of Purim, celebrated even today, sets the seal upon the accuracy of the story. This joyful feast celebrates a deliverance of the Jews from a mass murder in Persia. It was a Thanksgiving Day for the chosen people. Although they had forsaken God, He had spared them. Deliverance seems to be the keynote of Jewish history. God has always delivered this nation from danger and servitude. Even yet, God will deliver His people in the hour of their trouble.

This Book of Esther is an important link in a chain of events that tell of the re-establishment of the Hebrew nation in their own land in preparation of the coming of the Messiah into the world. The Jews had escaped extermination. It was God's purpose that they should be preserved to bring forth the Saviour of the world.

DON'T FORGET . . .

1. Do what is right and leave the rest with God. (Esther 4:16)
2. God has placed you in the world at this time for a purpose. (Esther 4:14)
3. Prayer moves the hand that moves the world. A

devoted maiden moved a determined monarch. (Ps. 76:10)

4. Those who walk in holy sincerity with Christ may walk in holy security among men.

5. God's pioneers leave all—to gain all. They are expendables.

QUIZ OF ESTHER

Does the teaching of Christ make a difference in the social and moral life of a nation? Compare the social and moral life of Esther's day with ours.

It does not seem possible that in our civilized age that anything could happen as cruel as the mass persecution of the Jews that Haman suggested. Do you think that the persecution of the Jews by the Nazis and the "purges" of World War II had the same earmarks of cruelty?

Was this barbaric cruelty of World War II carried on by heathen nations? Has culture and education changed the hearts of men? God tells us that the natural heart is desperately wicked.

God has a plan for every person. What was God's plan for Esther? How did she fulfill God's plan? (Esther 4:14-16)

Have you discovered God's plan for your life? Does God call only on those who are going into the ministry or missionary work, etc., or does God call men into business, teaching, farming, nursing and the like? In what professions or vocations are you interested? Can you serve God in these professions?

God always has someone in reserve to fulfill His purposes. Sometimes it is a man like Joseph, or Moses. Sometimes it is a woman like Hannah, or Esther, or Mary. Recall men in history whom God seems to have prepared and kept for the hour.

Discuss Esther as an expendable. Answer the question personally; am I an expendable?

What was wrong with Haman's well thought out plans?

STRICTLY PERSONAL

Do not pray for an easy task. Pray to be stronger!

The greatness of a man's power is the measure of his surrender. It is not a question of who you are, or of what you are, but whether God controls you.

"I wholly followed the Lord." (Caleb)

Be sure—be sure—be sure! Your sin will find you out.

God commands a complete out and out for Him.

Facts do not change; feelings do.

It is not enough to light a fire; you must put fuel on it.

It is never right to do wrong!

Minimum Daily Requirements / Spiritual Vitamins

Sunday: REJECTION OF VASHTI Esther 1
Monday: CROWNING OF ESTHER Esther 2
Tuesday: PLOTTING OF HAMAN Esther 3; 4
Wednesday: VENTURE OF ESTHER Esther 5
Thursday: MORDECAI EXALTED Esther 6
Friday: ESTHER'S FEAST Esther 7; 8
Saturday: DELIVERANCE OF THE JEWS Esther 9; 10

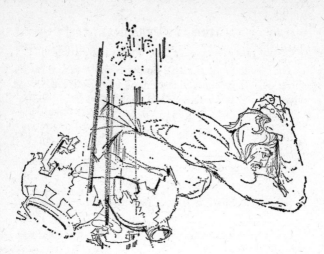

Chapter 15

LET'S LOOK AT JOB

JOB PORTRAYS JESUS CHRIST,
OUR REDEEMER

Read this book as you would read any thrilling story and be able to tell it.

The chief subject of the Book of Job is the riddle of all times, "Why do the righteous suffer, or why do the innocent suffer unjustly?"

Trials and suffering are not always for our punishment but sometimes for our education and training. The athlete is not put under strict discipline for punishment but merely to make him ready for the race. Christ is ever preparing us for the race that is set before us. (See Hebrews 12:1,2.)

The Book of Job tells us much about human suffering. Job's friends, as thousands do today, made the mistake of thinking that all suffering is God's way of punishing sin. They asked, *Who ever perished, being innocent* (Job 4:7)?

Do you know of any good person today who is suffering? Of course you do. One of the greatest saints I ever knew was blind; another was so poor that we, as children, carried him things to eat and saved our money to buy him clothes. We gave material things to him, but he gave spiritual blessings to us.

Job's friends concluded that Job must have sinned greatly to account for such exceptional suffering. In reality God was to glorify Himself through the suffering of Job. How honored Job was to be allowed to suffer for God's sake. The Lord revealed some great truths to Job.

Although the Bible is not to teach science, its language is abreast of latest discoveries. Let us see some.

He . . . hangeth the earth upon nothing (Job 26:7).

What could better describe the law of gravity? Ancients had absurd ideas—some believing the world was supported by a turtle, others, by Atlas' broad back. The "foundation" of the earth, thought to be stationary, was shown to Job to be literally "nothing."

Canst thou bind . . . Pleiades . . . (Job 38:31).

The Hebrew word evidently refers to the cluster of stars called Pleiades. Photographic plates show the principal stars as enveloped and threaded together by delicate streams of nebulous matter.

The morning stars sang together (Job 38:7). (See Psalm 19:1-3.)

Modern science has discovered that light rays have sound and that if our ears were more finely tuned, we could hear them.

. . . Green before the sun . . . (Job 8:16).

Our humble yardful of grass is the scene of a wonderful chemical process by which each blade is transformed from pale yellow to deep green as chlorophyl is absorbed from the sun. Overturn a board left lying on the grass—notice the nearly white blades. Return in a few days and you will see them turning "green before the sun."

. . . The circuit of heaven . . . (Job 22:14).

Scientists for years taught that the world was flat. Some today, ignorant of Scripture, accuse the Bible of nourishing this error. The Bible, however, is the only ancient book stating the truth concerning the earth's shape thousands of years before astronomers discovered it. The "circuit of heaven" is the "sphere" of heaven. Isaiah 40:22 mentions "the circle of the earth." The earth's sphericity is scripturally confirmed. Mathematical measurements are hinted at in Job 38:4-6.

. . . Canst thou guide Arcturus (Job 38:32)?

Arcturus is the fastest moving star which we can see without a telescope. It moves at the rate of seventy-five miles per second or 4,500 miles a minute.

. . . Weight for the winds; . . . waters by measure (Job 28:25).

Air-weight and water-weight are accepted facts—accepted now, revealed scripturally 2000 B.C., 3643 years before Galileo discovered them. Air's weight, 15 pounds to the square inch at sea level, alone is proper for life. "Waters" were measured and weighed by God. Scientists agree that earth's water-content could not be appreciably increased or lessened without destroying life. (See also Job 38:8-11.)

By what way is the light parted (Job 38:24)?

When the spectrum is taken of white light there is

nearly an unlimited number of lines produced; each one may be said to represent a different color.

Hast thou entered into the springs of the sea (Job 38:16)?

It was only after man had invented suitable equipment for exploring the ocean's floor that the amazing fact of "springs of the sea," mentioned here, was discovered.

. . . Treasures of the snow . . . (Job 38:22).

Modern photography now is revealing the fantastic and remarkably mathematical shapes of snow. Perfect crystals, each differing from the other, declare the wisdom and power of their Creator.

The face of the deep is frozen (Job 38:30).

Water cooling and freezing are shown here. Physicists recall that cooling liquids condense, become heavier. But at 4° Centigrade, condensation ceases, and weight is stabilized. Ice then begins to expand and grow lighter, forming a covering and protection for life in the waters.

Job never really saw himself until he saw God. This is true of every life.

Listen to God speak of Job. *Shall he that contendeth with the Almighty instruct him* (Job 40:2)? Think of trying to instruct the God of this universe! The wisdom of man is only foolishness with God. Hear Job's answer. *Behold, I am vile* [absolutely worthless]; *. . . I will lay mine hand upon his mouth* (Job 40:4).

God kept dealing with Job till he came to the very end of himself! Hear Job speak again, *Have I uttered that I understood not; things too wonderful for me, which I knew not . . . I have heard of thee by the hearing of the ear: but now mine eye seeth thee. Wherefore I abhor myself, and repent in dust and ashes* (Job 42:3,5,6).

We find Job a chastened, softened servant. God turns the tide and his prosperity is given back to him doubled—twice as many sheep and oxen, asses and camels! He rejoiced again in his sons and daughters, just the same number as before.

Job no longer asks a question but makes a statement. *I know that my redeemer liveth, and that he shall stand at the latter day upon the earth: and though after my skin worms destroy this body, yet in my flesh shall I see God* (Job 19:25,26).

We had heard him asking a question that multitudes have asked, *If a man die, shall he live again* (Job 14:14)? Paul answers this question in the great resurrection chapter of the Bible, I Corinthians 15. Jesus answers it in His statement, *He that believeth in me, though he were dead, yet shall he live* (John 11:25).

As the book opens we see Job surrounded by wealth, family, position and friends. Let us watch this man who God said was upright! We see this man visited by Satan. A swift succession of calamities follow. Remember these things did not come because of anything wrong in this man Job. All of Job's friends thought that the reason for his trouble lay in himself. But God had made it very plain in the opening of the book that this was not true.

Watch this man stripped of his wealth and reduced to poverty! His children are taken! Health is gone! Then he loses the confidence of his wife! Finally his friends go!

JOB AND SATAN (Read Job 1:6–2:10)

The scene opens with the gathering of the "sons of God" presenting themselves before the King. Satan is among them.

God speaks to Satan, *Whence comest thou?* What a tragedy in the answer: *From going to and fro in the* earth, and from walking up and down in it. This reveals the "endless restlessness of evil." *Be sober, be vigilant; because your adversary the devil, as a roaring lion, walketh about, seeking whom he may devour* (I Peter 5:8).

God speaks again, *Hast thou considered my servant Job* (Job 1:8).

What do you think God meant by "considering" Job? It is a strong word, as if he had been watching his every act. "Have you been trying to find a flaw?"

Satan says, *Doth Job fear God for nought?* He seems to imply—"I'm trying to find out why this fellow is so perfect. There is a reason." *Hast not thou made an hedge about him, . . . and about all that he hath on every side?* That was the truth, of course. Then he added, *thou hast blessed the work of his hands.* This was true also. *And his substance is increased in the land.* Yes, all this was correct.

But Satan went on, *But put forth thine hand now, and touch all that he hath, and he will curse thee to thy face.* Satan's charge against Job was that a man only serves God for what he can get out of it. Really Job is not so much on trial here as God. Job's loyalty was not so much in question as God's power. Is God able to keep *that which we have committed unto him* (II Tim. 1:12)?

This same thing is being said today! Some say that ministers are preaching the gospel for what they can get out of it; that heathens are turning to Christ because it gives them food and shelter.

So God says, "All right, try it out! Take everything away from Job and see what happens!"

The real conflict was between God and Satan. God was proving that Satan's statement concerning His children was a lie, that is, that they only serve Him for what they can get out of it.

149

When the trials came, Job did not understand the meaning of all his suffering. He knew it was not because he had sinned, as his friends said. He wondered what God was doing. We will not always understand what God is working out on the battleground of our hearts. But know this: There is a reason and value to everything that God allows. (Romans 8:28)

Don't always try to find the reason for your trials and experiences. Sometimes we will have to wait for the answer. We wonder why a Borden of Yale dies when he is only a young man at the threshold of a life of service, and an old drunken, apparently good-for-nothing is allowed to live.

Do not be surprised to find hypocrites in every congregation of God's children. Satan comes to do mischief to saints. He sets us to criticizing. He sows dissensions in the congregation. He distracts our attention. He excites the pride of preachers and singers, of givers and those who publicly pray. He chills our spirit, and freezes our prayers. Yes, when the Word is being sown, the fowls of the air come to pluck it away.

Remember, you can never walk before God and try to lead a godly life, without Satan coming in to walk with you—accusing you, finding fault and vexing you.

Luther was in great danger of being stabbed by a Jew. A friend sent him the picture of the assassin, and so he was put on his guard. If we know the adversary and are acquainted with his wiles, he cannot pounce upon us in our devotions, in our prayer, and in our walk; for we will not be "ignorant of his devices."

JOB AND HIS FRIENDS (Read Job 2:11–37:24)

Get acquainted with Job's friends. Let us introduce you to them. First there is courtly Eliphaz, then argumentative Bildad, and blunt Zophar, and the youthful Elihu.

This is a familiar scene. Job's four friends came. Do you know Job was rich in friends? Generally when a man loses his wealth and position and health, he has no friends left.

They wished to tell Job why they thought he was suffering as he did. They all agreed that he must have sinned miserably to have caused this suffering.

Eliphaz backs his argument by a dream (Job 4:1–5:27); Bildad, by some old proverbs (Job 8); Zophar, by experience and reason (Job 11). Elihu came nearest the truth when he argued that suffering was God's discipline to bring the soul back into fellowship with God; but it was not the whole truth.

God called Job "perfect and upright." His friends were wrong in charging him with sin as the only possible cause of his calamities.

The chief question returns: "Why does God permit the righteous to suffer?"

Job cries out from the ashes, "I cannot understand it. It doesn't seem right."

Job's wife, looking on discouraged, says, "Something is wrong. Your religion is a failure. Curse God and die." This literally means, "Say goodbye to God." It is the voice of despair.

Eliphaz adds, shaking his head, "God never makes a mistake. What have you done to bring this on yourself?"

Bildad says, "God is just. Confess your sin."

Zophar next speaks, "God is all wise. He knows man."

Elihu, God's man, says the wisest thing, "God is good; look up, and trust Him, for He is God."

Jehovah now is heard from the whirlwind as if to confirm Elihu, *I am God, and beside me there is none else.*

Now Job speaks himself: "Lord, Thou art God; Thou doest all things well. I will trust and not be afraid." Then comes the great confession, *I have heard of thee by the hearing of the ear: but now mine eye seeth thee. Wherefore I abhor myself* [count myself out], *and repent in dust and ashes* (Job 42:5,6).

This is the voice of victory. When we bow to God's will, we find God's way. Stoop to conquer. Bend to obey. This is the lesson of Job.

The philosophy of Job's friends was wrong. Job was glad to see them and he could pour out his troubles to them, but they did not understand him.

Job even lost his friends! He had tried to explain, but he was misunderstood. God only understands!

JOB AND JEHOVAH (Read Job 38–42)

As so often is true with us, when Job came into the presence of God, he forgot the speech he thought he would make! (Job 40:4,5) There was no arguing with God. Finally, Job went flat down on his face, repenting in "dust and ashes." (Job 42:6) This is the only place to learn God's lessons—on your face, with your mouth shut! It was here that Paul also came—and he gives us the conclusion of the matter in Philippians 3:4-9. There he counts the loss of "all things" as nothing, and then discovers a new righteousness *which is through the faith of Christ*. The place of true righteousness is there at the place of humility, with Paul, Job, and Jehovah.

Jehovah explains to Job that when men see God something always happens. The godly are allowed to suffer that they may see themselves. Read Isaiah 6:1-5. When Isaiah saw himself as he really was, he fell on his face undone and cried out, *I am a man of unclean lips.*

Did you ever think that you looked all right until some friend dropped in to invite you to go some place with him? When you saw how immaculate your friend looked, you immediately realized how you needed a good grooming. So often this is true in the presence of Christ. The very immaculateness of His Person makes us feel sinful. Measure your life by His life and you will feel as Job did.

As you read the account, you see that Job enjoyed a double portion of prosperity from the hand of God.

God allows His children to suffer in order to reveal character, to set forth an object lesson, and to bring to light some hidden sin. In Job's case, that hidden sin was self-righteousness.

This book well illustrates the text of Romans 8:28. How wonderful to hear of the patience of Job and to have seen how that the end of the Lord is pity and mercy. A morning of joy always follows the night of sorrow.

Job found God in his trouble. Many know God as a creator and believe in His greatness, but they do not really know God. The more we understand His ways the more we love and trust Him.

Job is rich in gems of spiritual truth. Underline the following references: Job 1:21; 5:17; 13:15; 14:14; 16:21; 19:23-27; 23:10; 26:7-14; 28:12-28; 42:1-6. These are some of the most frequently quoted and best loved passages in the Bible.

QUIZ OF JOB

When we try to do our best and live wisely, does everything turn out all right in our life? What kind of man was Job? (1:1,8)

What tragedies did Job suffer?

What reason did Job's friends give for his suffering? Were they right? What did God say about Job? (Job 1)

Do you ever sing, "Spirit of the Living God, fall afresh on me. Melt me; mold me; fill me; use me"? Do you know what it might mean for you?

God demonstrates His power and wisdom when He asks Job questions about the universe which no man can answer.

Man will never find the answer to all of God's dealings. Men may be honest and sincere as far as they go, as were Job's friends, but God's ways are past finding out. What did Job discover in all of this? (Job 19:25,26)

What were Job's words of trust in his God? (Job 13:15)

Minimum Daily Requirements / Spiritual Vitamins
Sunday: SATAN AND SAINT Job 1:1, 2—2:13
Monday: BILDAD THINKS JOB A HYPOCRITE Job 8:1-22
Tuesday: JOB ANSWERS HIS FRIENDS Job 12:1-25
Wednesday: JOB'S FAITH Job 19:1-29
Thursday: JOB AND ELIHU Job 32:1-22; 37:23, 24
Friday: GOD SPEAKS TO JOB Job 38:1-18
Saturday: JOB VINDICATED AND HONORED Job 42:1-17

Chapter 16

LET'S LOOK AT PSALMS

PSALMS PORTRAYS JESUS CHRIST,
OUR ALL IN ALL

The Psalms is the National Hymn Book of Israel. It contains one hundred and fifty poems to be set to music for worship. Worship is the central idea. The Psalms magnify and praise the Lord, exalt His attributes, His names, His word, and His goodness. Every human experience is related to Him.

We see the life of the believer pictured in all of its experiences of joy and sorrow, victory and failure. With what Psalms are you familiar? Pause a moment to think.

In Psalms we have the Christian on his knees.

In Proverbs we have the Christian on his feet.

The Psalms are full of Christ. He said, *All things must be fulfilled, which were written in the . . . psalms, concerning me* (Luke 24:44). They tell of Christ's:

Prophetic office in 22:22.
Priestly office in 40:6, 8; 22; 49; 110.
Kingly office in 2; 21; 45; 72.
Sufferings in 22 and 69.
Resurrection in 16.

We speak of the Psalms as the Psalms of David. He has been considered the principal writer. He gives the keynote and his voice rises highest in the sacred choir. But there were other authors in addition to him. Seventy-three of the one hundred and fifty psalms are assigned to him, and fifty are anonymous. The ninetieth Psalm is by Moses. Two are by Solomon, the seventy-second and one hundred and twenty-seventh. Besides these, Asaph, David's choir leader, the sons of Korah, a family of official musicians, and Jeduthun wrote some. But let us not be too disturbed in finding who penned them. Let us rather read and enjoy these grand expressions of praise. They are of God, for you. Sing them and make them your own. Catch David's note and spirit. He had marching songs, prayer songs, rally songs, hilltop songs, confession songs. Sing as you march. Keep step with David and David's Lord all the way.

MAN, HIS STATE OF BLESSEDNESS, FALL, AND RECOVERY (Read Psalms 1–41)

In this section we have a collection of David's Psalms.

Psalm 1 tells us of the road to success. Everyone

wants to prosper. No one wishes to fail. The psalmist says, "Everybody may prosper." Think of it! It will be well for every person to master the rules for success laid down here.

1. Things Not to Do

Refuse to walk in the counsel of the ungodly; do not take their advice or follow their pattern.

Refuse to stand in the way of sinners. When you do, it shows that you have been brought under the spell of evil.

Refuse to sit in the seat of the scornful. This is the most despicable place possible. The scorner is sure "that every minister, missionary, or Christian worker is either a fool or a hypocrite."

2. Things to Do

Read the Bible.
Delight in it.
Meditate upon it.

The more you read the Word the more you want to. As one great Christian leader has said, "The Gospel feeds you, then it makes you hungry." It never grows stale. You cannot read it too often or too much.

3. Things That Result

When the Christian has followed the "don'ts" and "do's" of Psalm 1, what are the three results in his life?

"Planted"—*like a tree planted* [transplanted] *by the rivers of water*—steadfast in a luxuriant soil.

"Purposeful"—he *bringeth forth his fruit in his season*—the productive life.

"Prosperous"—*his leaf also shall not wither*—the abiding, happy life.

Other Psalms in this group that show the final blessings of man because of the glorious work of the "Man Christ Jesus" are Psalms 22, 23, 24.

Psalm 23

This is the most loved of all the psalms. Every child learns it and every aged one facing death finds his comfort there. Dr. Hodgkin says, "It contains three secrets: the secret of a happy life, a happy death, and a happy eternity."

We call this the Shepherd's Psalm and so it is but we see that the psalm before it and after it have great bearing upon the twenty-third.

Psalm 22 tells of the Good Shepherd giving His life for His sheep. We see the cross and hear the cries of our dying Saviour.

Psalm 23 tells of the great Shepherd keeping His sheep. We read *The Lord is my shepherd; I shall not want.* He promises to guide, provide and keep me.

Psalm 24 tells of the chief Shepherd in His glory rewarding His sheep. He is my King and He is coming to reign in power and great glory.

COMPARE THESE VERSES:

Psalm 22:1 . . . . Matthew 27:46

Psalm 22:6,7 . . . . Luke 23:35,36

Psalm 22:6-8 . . . . Matthew 27:39,41,43

Psalm 22:12,13 . . . . Matthew 27:36,44

Psalm 22:28 . . . . I Cor. 15:23,24

In Psalm 22 we find a picture of Calvary: *poured out like water . . . my heart is like wax; it is melted* (Psalm 22:14). This describes excessive perspiration due to physical torture. It also means the breaking of Jesus' heart. He tells why His heart was broken. *Reproach hath broken my heart.* (Psalm 69:20). *But one of the soldiers with a spear pierced his side, and forthwith came there out blood and water. And he that saw it bare record, and his record is true: and he knoweth that he saith true, that ye might believe* (John 19:34,35).

Jesus died of a broken heart. He bore the reproach and shame for others. The bearing of our sins which hid Him from His Father's face, broke His heart. Death by a broken heart is very rare. It is caused by intense agony.

My tongue cleaveth to my jaws (Psalm 22:15). This verse describes intense thirst. The account in the New Testament said, *Jesus . . . that the scripture might be fulfilled, saith, I thirst.* Yes, Psalm 69:21 says, *In my thirst they gave me vinegar to drink.* Read John 19:28, 29.

They pierced my hands and my feet (Psalm 22:16). These words give the description of death by crucifixion—*bones out of joint*—bones of hands, arms, shoulders out of joint due to nailing to the cross and straining of bone and muscle. This was the Roman method of death. The Jew did not know of this.

They part my garments among them, and cast lots upon my vesture (Psalm 22:18). Even the act of the soldiers is described here. See Matthew 27:35.

ISRAEL (Read Psalms 42–72)

This section opens with a "cry" from the depth of oppression. See Psalms 42–49. It ends with the King reigning over the redeemed nation. *He shall have dominion also from sea to sea, and from the river unto the ends of the earth* (Psalm 72:8). Read this glorious psalm.

There are several psalms of penitence, but the chief is David's Psalm 51. In II Samuel 11 and 12, you find the story of David's sin.

David confessed and said, *I have sinned against the Lord* (II Sam. 12:13). That is what sin is—breaking God's law.

You notice in Psalm 51 these words, *Against thee,*

thee only, have I sinned, and done this evil in thy sight.
Sin is against God.

We learn from this Psalm that we must confess our sin to God; (See I John 1:9.) that God is just to forgive. Whenever a man is sincere in his confession to God, He will forgive his sin.

THE SANCTUARY (Read Psalms 73–89)

In these Psalms we see the sanctuary mentioned, or referred to, in almost every one of this third section. (See Psalm 84:1.) It is concerned almost entirely with material used in worship service, and needs little comment.

THE EARTH (Read Psalms 90–106)

The first of this group of Psalms was written during the wanderings in the wilderness and a collection was made by Ezra and Nehemiah.

Read the opening verses of Psalms 90 and 91 together. *Lord, thou hast been our dwelling place in all generations. . . . He that dwelleth in the secret place of the most High shall abide under the shadow of the Almighty.* If God is our dwelling place on this earth, we shall live at peace, sheltered by the Almighty. Christ says, *If ye abide in me, and my words abide in you, ye shall ask what ye will, and it shall be done unto you* (John 15:7). The secret of a godly life is abiding in the Almighty. When the devil attacked the Lord, he quoted from Psalm 91. But Christ was victorious because He lived in the place described by this same psalm. We are told that there is a point of perfect calm at the center of a cyclone. There may be raging stormy snares, pestilences, terror by night, darkness and destruction, but when the soul is abiding under the shadow of the Almighty, it is safe.

These chapters are more things to be *done* than *read*.

If you wish to praise the Lord for His goodness, read Psalm 103. It is full of worship, adoration, praise and thanksgiving. This is great exercise for the soul.

This is a great psalm to commit to memory. Repeat it often for "praise is comely for the upright."

THE WORD OF GOD (Read Psalms 107–150)

All the teaching in these psalms is grouped around the Word of God.

This section opens with Psalm 107 which gives the key. *He sent His word, and healed them* (verse 20).

Psalm 119 is the great Psalm of the whole book. It extols the Word of God which is the great revelation of the heart and mind of the Lord. Almost every verse speaks of God's Word, or law, or precepts.

The value of the Psalms to us depends upon our need. Spurgeon said, "The trail is full of meaning to the Indian, for his quick eye knows how to follow it; it would not mean a tenth as much to a white man. The sight of the lighthouse is cheering to the mariner, for from it he gathers his whereabouts." So will those who are in need spiritually lay hold on the songs of David and prize them and live upon them.

Praise is the highest duty that any creature can discharge. "Man's chief end is to glorify God." There is no heaven either here or in the world to come for people who do not praise God. If you do not enter into the spirit and worship of heaven, the spirit and joy of heaven cannot enter you!

The Psalms begin with the word "blessed." This word is multiplied in this book. The book seems to be built around this first word. There is not one "woe" in the entire Psalms.

Hold your Bible in your hand and turn to the middle of the book. It is the Psalms. Not merely is this true physically. There is a deeper truth. It is central also in human experience.

It is the book for all who are in need, the sick and suffering, the poor and needy, the prisoner and exile, the man in danger, the persecuted. It is a book for the sinner, telling him of God's great mercy and forgiveness. It is a book for the child of God, leading him into new experiences with the Lord. It tells of God's law in its perfection and pronounces blessings upon the one who will keep it.

WORLD'S LARGEST ORCHESTRA EXCLUSIVELY RELIGIOUS

Drawing from the largest orchestra personnel ever to be set aside for a specific purpose, David, famed hymnist and concert harpist, devotes much of his time to adorning the worship of God by managing sacred sanctuary symphonies. Nothing but religious music is used. The Jewish Chronicles report *four thousand praised the LORD with the instruments which I* [David] *made* (I Chron. 23:5).

NATIONAL HYMN BOOK FOR JEWISH PEOPLE RELEASED

Under the batons, principally of the famous Asaph family, Jewish choral music has reached a peak of unusual eminence. To provide their people with marching songs for their annual pilgrimages to the Passover feast, "Pilgrim Psalms" (120–134) were arranged and published for the journeys themselves. The "Hallel" or "Praise" Psalms are reserved for use at the feast proper. (Psalms 113–118)

Astronomy in the Psalms

When I consider thy heavens, the work of thy fingers, the moon and the stars, which thou hast ordained; what is man, that thou art mindful of him? and the son of man, that thou visitest him? (Psalm 8:3,4)

These words express the wonders of modern astronomy. Today when scientists see our place among the infinities of this universe, they raise the cry, "Is it conceivable that the God of this universe would be concerned about such an insignificant speck as this earth, such a small thing in His vast creation?" David said the same thing in his day, anticipating the wonders which scientific knowledge had not yet revealed.

His going forth is from the end of the heaven, and his circuit unto the ends of it: and there is nothing hid from the heat thereof. (Psalm 19:6)

This tells of the movement of the sun in the heavens. It goes forth "as a strong man to run a race." "His circuit is unto the ends of it." None of the ancients knew the movement of the sun. This is a comparatively modern discovery. Now we know it is "running" through the heavens at the speed of about twelve and a half miles per second and its "circuit" is so great that in 250,000 years the distance traveled is too negligible to measure.

He causeth the vapors to ascend from the ends of the earth; he maketh lightnings for the rain; he bringeth the wind out of his treasuries. (Psalm 135:7) (Read Ecclesiastes 1:7.)

This describes the facts of absorption and condensation of water from the sea into clouds and then into rain. This establishes the equilibrium of water on land and sea. In Psalms we see the vapor rising from the ocean to the sky. No pumps could accomplish such a feat. In the cold upper air the vapor condenses and is held in clouds. If left there the water will fall on the sea. Psalm 135:7 tells us how this is averted. God has a way. "He bringeth the wind out of His treasuries." The clouds are borne silently to the mountains. (See Psalm 104:8,9.) How will they become rain? "He prepareth the lightnings for the rain." This shock precipitates the rain. Lord Kelvin said, "I believe there never is rain without lightning." The psalmist, inspired by God, stated accurately in his day what scientists are discovering today.

QUIZ OF PSALMS

We call the Psalms the National Hymn Book of Israel. They express the spiritual experiences of the people. The Negro has music which expresses his own experiences of joy and sorrow. What Negro spirituals do you know? "Nobody Knows the Trouble I've Seen," "Swing Low, Sweet Chariot," "Lord, I Want to Be a Christian," etc. Can you add others?

What are some of the hymns of the Reformation? The hymns of our own country? Talk to your choirmaster about the hymns of the church.

Are we producing great hymns in America today? Most of our experiences today are not spiritual. We are living in the age of science, the H bomb, etc. This does not inspire hymnology.

The Psalms are for worship. Paul says to worship with psalms and hymns and spiritual songs. Do you think that most people today really go to church to worship or to "hear good music" and "a good sermon"?

Think over the worship service of your own church. Are there many men in your church service? Many young people? How can you contribute to the spirit of worship?

What Psalms speak of Christ?

Recall the facts of astronomy in Psalms.

What are your favorite Psalms? Why? Do they express your spiritual feelings?

How is Christ portrayed in Psalms?

Minimum Daily Requirements / Spiritual Vitamins

Sunday: PSALMS OF LAW Psalms 1; 19

Monday: PSALMS OF CREATION Psalms 29; 104

Tuesday: PSALMS OF JUDGMENT Psalms 52; 53

Wednesday: PSALMS OF CHRIST Psalms 22; 40; 41

Thursday: PSALMS OF LIFE Psalms 3; 31

Friday: PSALMS OF THE HEART Psalms 37; 42

Saturday: PSALMS OF GOD Psalms 90; 139

Chapter 17

LET'S LOOK AT PROVERBS, ECCLESIASTES, SONG OF SOLOMON

*PORTRAYS JESUS CHRIST,
OUR WISDOM; THE END OF ALL LIVING;
THE LOVER OF OUR SOULS*

Proverbs is a book for everyday instruction. It deals with the practical affairs of life. We find our duty to God, our neighbors, the duty of parents and children, and our obligations as citizens. The author, Solomon, wrote more wisely than he lived. Solomon wrote four hundred years before the seven wise men of Greece. This book divides men into two classes—wise and foolish.

Wisdom is the important word in this book. It means more than an excellent attribute. The Wisdom of Proverbs is the incarnate Word of the New Testament. Christ found Himself in this book. (Luke 24:27)

Wisdom is represented as dwelling with God from all eternity. *I was set up from everlasting, from the beginning, or ever the earth was . . . When he prepared the heavens, I was there: when he set a compass upon the face of the depth: . . . when he appointed the foundations of the earth: then I was by him, as one brought up with him* [I was as His artificer]. (See Proverbs 8:23-31.) Compare these verses with John 1:1,2; Hebrews 1:2; Colossians 2:3.

When you read the Book of Proverbs put *Christ* instead of *wisdom* in the verse. (See I Cor. 1:30.) You will see a wonderful power in this book. *And we know that the Son of God is come, and hath given us an understanding, that we may know him that is true* (I John 5:20).

The Bible is a book on woman's rights. Proverbs closes with woman's chapter, Proverbs 31. *Give her of the fruit of her hands; and let her own works praise her in the gates.* Wherever Christ goes, womanhood is lifted up. In heathen countries, woman is never more than a chattel or slave. In Christian lands, woman is treated like a queen.

God wants to give us of His wisdom—the wisdom which created heavens and earth, that we might use it in all of life. (James 1:5) This would put an end to all the confusion and evil in this world, wouldn't it? Human wisdom can never solve life's problems. Only God knows the ways of men. "The fear of the Lord is the beginning of wisdom."

COUNSEL FOR YOUNG MEN (Read Proverbs 1–10)
Sermons for Sons

"WISE UP!" Worship is the first step to wisdom. (1:7)

"WALK STRAIGHT!" The "straight and narrow" has the lowest accident rate. (2:20)

"DIRECTIONS" Ask God about everything; He knows every road. (3:6)

"WATCH YOUR STEP!" Every step helps mould character. (4:26)

"FLEE FLATTERY" "Smoother than oil" is modern terminology. (5:3)

"GOD'S BLACK-LIST" Pride, lies, murder, deceit, mischief, betrayal, discord. (6:17,18,19)

"A BAD WOMAN" Read carefully Proverbs 7:5-27.

"RICHES" Rubies of wisdom command highest prices on the character market. (8:11)

"MORE FUN" Nothing you ought not to do is ever "more fun." Wait till you see what happens. (9:17)

"WANTED! SILENCE" Wordy men seldom are wise men. (10:19)

We find the whole body included: Proverbs 4:23-26.

"Keep thy heart" . . . . Verse 23
"Put away a forward mouth" . . . . Verse 24
"Let thine eyes look right on" . . . . Verse 25
"Ponder the path of thy feet" . . . . Verse 26

The duty of parents to chastise their children is based upon God's chastening of His children. (Proverbs 3:11, 12) One of the signs of the last wicked days is given by Paul as "disobedient to parents." (II Timothy 3:2) What happened to Eli and his boys because he allowed his sons to sin? (See I Samuel 4:15-18.)

There are many sins of the tongue. We use it too freely. We lie and are deceitful in dealings with others. Much is said about guarding the tongue, for in the tongue is the power of life and death. (Proverbs 12:22; 18:21)

We find the author pleading with us to shun evil companions, pride, envy, intemperance, sins of the tongue and idleness. (See Proverbs 1:10-19; 4:14-19; also chapters 3; 10; 13; 15; 16; 18; 19.)

All these things would be impossible to do unless we had Christ, the Wisdom of God, within us. The old Spartan tried to make a corpse stand upright. He found that it would always fall. "Alas, it needs something inside!" he said. Yes, this corpse needed life. So we that would obey these injunctions of life need Christ. He will live through us. He will keep us and guard us and make the impossible, the possible in our lives.

Read about pride and its consequences in Proverbs 8; 11; 16; 19. (See Proverbs 16:18.) The Lord wants us always to be humble before Him and not to esteem ourselves better than others. Every truly great person is humble.

SHUN SINNERS ALTOGETHER

My son, if sinners entice thee (Prov. 1:10)—and sinners will entice thee. What peril there is to the life of today from bad literature, bad companionships, bad habits! Only God knows how much.

My son, walk not thou in the way with them. (Prov. 1:15) You will feel lonesome sometimes. You will often be unpopular. Don't let that make you waver. Better be alone than in bad company!

Refrain thy foot from their path. (Prov. 1:15) There is a certain narrow road, much jeered at, much neglected, but on which there was never an accident and the end is heaven. Be truly wise; choose that.

COUNSEL FOR ALL MEN (Read Proverbs 11–20)

Messages for Men

"FALSE ECONOMY" A gift is never lost; only what is selfishly kept impoverishes. (11:24)

"FOOLS" You cannot convince a fool of his actions; only a wise man will accept rebuke. (12:15)

"LYING" Righteousness and lying are enemies. (13:5)

"ANSWERS THAT HEAL" Two people ought not get angry at the same time. (15:1)

"CLEAN SIN" A man deep in wickedness will invent "pretty names for sin." (Spurgeon) (16:2)

"TO WIN FRIENDS" A friendly man will have friends. (18:24)

"DRINK UP!" When you decide for strong drink, don't be surprised when it decides against you. (20:1)

There has never been a time when men did as well as they knew how. However imperfect their instructions, they have never lived up to them. The last thing a man could complain of is a lack of good advice.

A drunken man was holding himself up by the lamppost when a well meaning passerby stopped to counsel him. "Let me give you a bit of good advice," he began.

"Now-eh-don't," was the hiccoughing response. "That's just-eh-what I don't need. Why-eh, my friend, I'm the best advised-eh-man in the town."

And he spoke for a whole class of evil-doers. Why should they go wrong? Have not they been told a better way? Of course they have. The trouble is not there.

Who has heart trouble? Who has woe? Sorrow? Contentions? (Read Proverbs 23:29-35.) No sin is more severely denounced in Scripture than this of drunkenness. *Know ye not that the unrighteous shall not inherit the kingdom of God? . . . Nor thieves, nor covetous, nor drunkards, nor revilers, nor extortioners, shall inherit the kingdom of God* (I Cor. 6:9,10).

170

Proverbs is an intensely practical book, exposing a series of traps that would ensnare us.

COUNSEL FOR KINGS AND RULERS
(Read Proverbs 21–31)

Rules for Rulers

"SELF CONTROL" A guarded mouth makes for a serene soul. (21:23)

"REPUTATION" Choose a good name rather than great riches. Your name goes on; your wealth stops at death. (22:1)

"SOBERNESS" Red wine is colorful but calamitous. (23:31)

"COUNSEL" The sober judgment of a sane thinking group is more reliable than your own opinion. (24:6)

"WOMEN" Better solitude on top of the house than sojourning in the house with a nagging woman. (25:24)

"GOSSIP" Fire goes out when fuel gives out; scandal stops when mouths are stopped. (26:20)

"TOMORROW" There is never a tomorrow, only today. Get it done now. (27:1)

"UNDERSTANDING" Rank does not guarantee an understanding heart. (28:16)

"BRIBES" Seek justice and your land shall stand; accept bribes and it will fall. (29:4)

"SECURITY" A trust in God is the only safe and sound soul armor. (30:5)

THE BOOK OF ECCLESIASTES

CONFESSION (Read Ecclesiastes 1—7)

The great question: "Is life worth living?" is presented. Solomon has tested it to the full. No man could better do it or better tell it—and the answer he gives is not reassuring for the life that now is.

Wisdom—what better thing is there in all the world? Solomon was the wisest man. He knew everything worth knowing. "I gave my heart to know wisdom." Yet he was forced to cry out, "Vanity of vanities!" *For in much wisdom is much grief: and he that increaseth knowledge, increaseth sorrow* (Eccl. 1:18). This is always true of just earthly wisdom. Remember "the fear of the Lord is the beginning of real wisdom."

I said in mine heart, Go to now. I will prove thee with mirth, therefore enjoy pleasure: and, behold, this also is vanity (Eccl. 2:1). This is his deliberate conclusion. God made us all to be joyful. He has given us a thousand avenues of enjoyment. Let us not sacrifice true happiness for questionable pleasure. Always make your recreation a re-creation. Edison, the man who brought more to men to make them happy than almost any other, said he did not believe there was a happy man in this world. No, if a person is trying to find his happiness "under the sun" it soon fades away. But with Christ, there are joys eternal.

Philosophy had failed, so let merriment be tried. Music, dance, wine (not to excess), the funny story, the clever repartee: these were now cultivated. Clowns were now welcomed to the court, where only grave philosophy had been. The halls of the palace resounded with laughter and gaiety. Yet, after a while, all this palled on the king's taste. He even went so far as to say that laughter was mad and mirth inane. (Eccl. 2:1-3)

Cheerfulness is admirable. A hearty laugh in its place is delightful but the person who is always giggling is a bore.

So he became practical. He attended to great works of state. Aqueducts, pools, palaces and other public buildings occupied his thoughts. Now the court fools were frowned upon and great architects were welcomed to the palace. But the excitement incident to building soon faded (Eccl. 2:4).

Vineyards, gardens, orchards, rare flowers, tropical plants were all the rage. Jerusalem and the vicinity bloomed like the Garden of Eden. Soon it was like a new toy for a child, that pleases for a while, but is soon tossed away (Eccl. 2:5,6).

Then the king tried cattle breeding, art collecting, and even became an amateur musician (v. 8). Choruses and orchestras gathered in the royal palace. But even though "music hath charms," it is powerless to charm permanently (Eccl. 2:7,8).

Try just living the weary round of life

Try living with discretion!—Eccl. 3 But again, "What profit?" (Eccl. 3:9) Vanity of vanities!

Try the stoic's philosophy!—Eccl. 4 Surely this also is vanity. He wails, *Vanity and vexation of spirit.* (Eccl. 4:16)

Try formal religion—Eccl. 5 Be sure to *pay that which thou hast vowed* (Eccl. 5:4). This, too, is vanity.

Try wealth!—Eccl. 6 Solomon had it. He was *a man to whom God hath given riches.* What is the good of it? *God giveth him not power to eat thereof, but a stranger eateth it: this is vanity, and it is an evil disease* (Eccl. 6:2). Many agree with Solomon in the emptiness of pleasures, but they think that money is the supreme goal in life. Jesus told us to seek first the kingdom of God and His righteousness, and all these things would be added.

We must learn that money cannot buy everything. A man was once walking down the street complaining bitterly that his feet were sore and he had no shoes, until he met a man who had no feet.

Try reputation!—Ecclesiastes 7 *A good name is better than precious ointment; and the day of death than the day of one's birth* (Eccl. 7:1). It doesn't last long in this world. Men are soon forgotten when they die. Vanity still!

ADMONITION (Read Ecclesiastes 8–12)

Now comes a turning point. Ecclesiastes 8:12 says, *Yet surely I know that it shall be well with them that fear God.* The full meaning of this is in the last chapter— *Fear God, and keep His commandments: for this is the whole duty of man* (Eccl. 12:13).

The phrase *under the sun* (Eccl. 1:3) is found twenty-eight times in this little book. The "under-the-sun-life" is hardly worth living; but above the sun, and in the heavenlies that Paul describes, it is glorious. (Ephesians 1)

We find in this book that we can never find satisfaction and happiness in this world. True happiness apart from Christ is impossible. We find dissatisfaction among the poor and rich alike, among the ignorant and learned, among people and kings.

Ecclesiastes closes with a call to the young! Lay the foundations early *Those that seek me early shall find me* (Prov. 8:17). This book is given as a danger sign, that we may be spared having to learn the bitterness of life by finding the cisterns we have sought to be empty. The greatest proportion of men and women who are living to serve God have chosen Him in childhood.

174

THE SONG OF SOLOMON

The Song of Solomon is an Oriental poem of love in marriage. This is a song of spiritual communion between the Bridegroom, representing Christ, and His bride, the church.

QUIZ OF PROVERBS, ECCLESIASTES, SONG OF SOLOMON

What Proverbs can apply to your own life?

How is Christ portrayed in Proverbs?

Most people today think that success and wealth and position will bring happiness. What does Ecclesiastes tell us? Is the writer correct in his conclusions?

How is Christ portrayed in Ecclesiastes?

How is Christ portrayed in the Song of Solomon?

Minimum Daily Requirements / Spiritual Vitamins

Sunday: GET WISDOM Proverbs 1–4

Monday: TO SONS Proverbs 5–7

Tuesday: GOOD AND BAD Proverbs 15–17

Wednesday: WISE WORDS Proverbs 20; 22; 31

Thursday: ALL IS VANITY Ecclesiastes 1–3

Friday: ONLY GOD SATISFIES Ecclesiastes 11; 12

Saturday: JOYFUL COMMUNION S. of Sol. 1:1-7; 2:1-7

Chapter 18

LET'S LOOK AT ISAIAH

ISAIAH PORTRAYS JESUS CHRIST,
THE MESSIAH

The prophets were men whom God raised up during the dark days of Israel's history. They were the evangelists of the day, the religious patriots of the hour.

We see Christ in this book and hear the prophet crying, "He is coming!" and "He is coming again!" He is coming as Saviour in humiliation as our sin-bearer, pictured in Isaiah 53. He is coming again in power and great glory, pictured in Isaiah 34.

As we look through the telescope, we see two mountain peaks with a valley between. One is called Calvary;

on its hilltop is a cross. But as we look farther we see another peak. It is radiant with the light of a crown! This hill is Olivet. The eye of the ancient seer went farther than the sufferings of Calvary; his eye caught the kingdom and the glory that should follow!

Yes, Christ, the Messiah is coming and He is coming again! This is what the Second Advent means. This is a glorious fact, our blessed hope. (See Isaiah 60:1; Acts 1:11; John 14:1-3.)

Isaiah speaks of Christ's death when he says, *though your sins be as scarlet, they shall be as white as snow; though they be red like crimson, they shall be as wool* (Isaiah 1:18). Again, *He is despised and rejected of men* (Isaiah 53:3). This speaks of the first time when He came unto his own, and his own received him not (John 1:11) but when He comes again we hear, *Arise, shine; for thy light is come, and the glory of the LORD is risen upon thee* (Isaiah 60:1). Then he tells us of His coming kingdom. *And it shall come to pass in the last days . . .* (Isaiah 2:2-5)

UNDER UZZIAH AND JOTHAM (Read Isaiah 1–6)

Read Isaiah 1:1 and you will discover that Isaiah was prophet during the reigns of Uzziah, Jotham, Ahaz and Hezekiah.

Isaiah warned Judah of her folly and rebellion. (Isaiah 1:2-9) They separated themselves from God by the sins of greed, heathen alliances, and idolatry. (Isaiah 2:6-9) God called them a fruitless vine. God had tried patience; now they must be destroyed by heathen kings.

God called Isaiah just as He called Moses, and Paul. Isaiah's commission came at the tragic death of the grand old King Uzziah. (Isaiah 6:1) It was a never-to-be-forgotten experience. It taught him his own unworthiness and gave him his real commission to a sinning, needy world. It came to him in the form of a "vision." Isaiah was the man of the hour. Let us look at the steps from the opening of the vision to his final commission.

This experience of Isaiah's should be every disciple's experience. The secret of all of Isaiah's power lay in this vision in the temple—"I saw the Lord!"

CONVICTION—*Woe is me . . . I am undone!* Sense of sinfulness before God's holiness. (Isaiah 6:5)

CONFESSION—*A man of unclean lips!* A broken and a contrite heart is precious to the Lord. (Isaiah 6:5)

CLEANSING—*Thy sin purged!* After confession, his lips cleansed. (Isaiah 6:7)

CONSECRATION—*Here am I; send me!* (Isaiah 6:8)

COMMISSION—*Go!* God's command. (Isaiah 6:9)

UNDER AHAZ (Read Isaiah 7–14)

Ahaz was utterly bad. He was an open idolater. For this sin God allowed Syria and Israel to invade his kingdom.

God sent the prophet to encourage Ahaz. (7:3) After predicting the Assyrian invasion in Isaiah 8, the prophet saw an end to all of Israel's troubles through the birth of the Christ child who shall rule over the kingdom of David in righteousness, forever and forever. He gave Ahaz a "sign" that Judah was not to perish— the prophecy of Immanuel, the Virgin's Son, Jesus Christ.

Read these important words in Isaiah 7:10-16. Ahaz refused this evidence. Then followed the sentence of doom upon king and land. (Isaiah 8:6-22) With nations, this is God's policy: doom for idolatry.

In Isaiah 9:6,7 we find another great prophecy

concerning Christ. Read it aloud! The Son to be given, the child to be born, was to sit on David's throne. Remember the "throne of David" is as definite as the "throne of the Caesars." Yes, Christ will sit on the throne of His father David. Hear the angel's words to Mary, *He shall be great, and shall be called the Son of the Highest: and the Lord God shall give unto him the throne of his father David: and he shall reign over the house of Jacob forever* (Luke 1:32,33).

In Isaiah 11 we see the picture of the glory of the future kingdom which Christ is coming to establish on this earth. He is coming to Jerusalem to sit upon the throne of David, and peace shall cover the earth *as the waters cover the sea.*

Read every word of Isaiah 11 and 12, which gives a picture of this coming King and kingdom.

1. The King Himself...................Isaiah 11:1
2. His anointing......................Isaiah 11:2
3. His righteous reign................Isaiah 11:3-5
4. His glorious kingdom...............Isaiah 11:6-9
5. His people gathered...............Isaiah 11:10-16
6. His kingdom worship................Isaiah 12

This is the kingdom that Christ came to this earth to establish, but they would not receive their King. (John 1:11; 19:15)

In Isaiah 13 we see great Babylon's doom. When it was my privilege to drive out to old Babylon and look over the ruins of that once magnificent city and see the absolute devastation, I thought of Isaiah's prophecy found in Isaiah 13:19-22 concerning this city. God said that *Babylon, the glory of kingdoms, the beauty of the Chaldees' excellency, shall be as when God overthrew Sodom and Gomorrah. It shall never be inhabited, neither shall it be dwelt in from generation to generation: neither shall the Arabian pitch tent there; neither*

179

shall the shepherds make their fold there. But wild
beasts of the desert shall lie there; and their houses
shall be full of doleful creatures; and owls shall dwell
there, and satyrs shall dance there. And the wild beasts
of the islands shall cry in their desolate houses, and
dragons in their pleasant palaces.

This is true today. There is not even the tent of an
Arab pitched there. Only bats and owls make their
home in its ruins. Not a shepherd is seen on the plains.
There is only desolation.

In Isaiah 14:28-32 we read that King Ahaz died. But
Isaiah warns the people that his death must not be
hailed as the end of their burdens. Even worse oppres-
sors than Ahaz were yet to come.

UNDER HEZEKIAH (Read Isaiah 15—66)

The reign of Hezekiah occupied one of the most
important periods in all of Israel's history. Hezekiah
was a godly king. The Assyrian armies, like a dark
storm cloud, were threatening the northern frontiers.
Before Hezekiah had completed his sixth year, Samaria
had fallen beneath this invader. This success only
whetted the Assyrian appetite for further conquest.
Eight years later Judah was invaded. The first invasion
was by Sargon and the second by his son, Sennacherib.
Assyrian history tells us this. The critical year in
Hezekiah's reign was the fourteenth. (Isaiah 36:1) It
was then we have the Assyrian invasion, the king's
mortal sickness and his recovery, and the final withdrawal of Assyrians from the land. (This covered four
years.)

These stony-hearted Assyrian warriors came year
after year, blazing with steel and banners. The watchmen on the walls of Jerusalem could see them advance
by the smoke of the burning towns.

King Hezekiah stripped the temple of its treasures

and took the gold from its doors and pillars in order that he might send them 300 talents of silver and 30 talents of gold to buy them off. (II Kings 18:13-16) In desperation help from Egypt was sought. But nothing availed.

Finally the Assyrians built their camp fires around the city of Jerusalem and demanded its surrender. Read the dramatic account of the parleyings between the Assyrian general and the Jerusalem chiefs.

See the account of the swift and terrible disaster that fell upon the enemy as they were slain by a mysterious visitation in their camp. (Isaiah 37:36-38)

Isaiah denounced the alliance with Egypt and said it was relying "on horses" and trusting *in chariots, because they are many; and in horsemen, because they are very strong* (Isaiah 31:1).

Today we have transferred our trust from "horses and chariots" to planes and projectiles, to missiles and the H-bomb. Now we have a rocket that is so powerful it will destroy all in its path, and with such a range that it can strike any place on earth. We are convinced that if this material were revised daily, it could not keep up with the great scientific strides of man. But without God it is a march of destruction.

We need to hear the prophet say today, *Woe to them that go down to Egypt for help; and stay on horses, and trust in chariots* (Isaiah 31:1). How great a need there is today for those who will remember the name of the Lord our God, who know *the saving strength of his right hand* (Psalm 20:6).

God wants us to recognize Him in national affairs. He calls His people to *turn ye unto him from whom the children . . . have deeply revolted* (Isaiah 31:6). As a people we must get right with God before we can get right with other nations. God was calling upon nations to repent of social and national conditions that brought on World War I—the injustice and class oppression, the national envy and fear, the godless materialism that were its roots, and before they changed, World War II had broken out in its fury.

The kingdoms of Judah and Israel had become so weakened by idolatry and corruption that the enemies swept down upon them from the north "like a wolf on the fold." First, Israel rolled in the dust under the tramp of the terrible Assyrian hosts (722 B.C.), and then Judah fell with the Babylonians thundering at her gate and breaking down her walls (586 B.C.). Both kingdoms ended and her people were carried into captivity. Isaiah lived and prophesied in Jerusalem.

Isaiah spent his life trying to get Israel to become acquainted with God and His Word. He wanted them to trust wholly in God's guidance. Isn't this a worthy aim for any minister today?

Chapters 46–66 of the book are called the "Book of Consolation" because Isaiah tells in glowing terms not only of the restoration of Judah but the coming of Jehovah's "Servant" to be the Messiah King. The restoration is assured for they must return to their own land to prepare the way for the coming Messiah, who is to redeem His people.

Isaiah 53 gives us a perfect picture of our suffering Redeemer. *Surely he hath borne our griefs, and carried our sorrows* (verse 4). *All we like sheep have gone astray; . . . and the LORD hath laid on him the iniquity of us all* (verse 6). He was the substitute for the sinner.

Can you repeat verse five and say, "He was wounded for my transgressions, He was bruised for my iniquities: the chastisement of my peace was upon Him; and with His stripes I am healed"? It is accepting this Messiah that makes you a child of God. He was wounded, bruised, pierced—not for His own sins, but for ours. He bore on His own body the sins of the world.

Isaiah 60–66 tells of the coming kingdom—the future glory of Israel. God's goodness to redeemed Israel is seen in chapters 61 and 62. He promises an era of prosperity in chapters 63-65.

QUIZ OF ISAIAH

What impresses you most about this prophet?

What was his message to Israel? to Judah?

What was his message before exile? after exile?

What judgments were pronounced?

What final blessings were pronounced?

How is Christ portrayed by this prophet?

Minimum Daily Requirements / Spiritual Vitamins

Sunday: GOD'S CASE AGAINST JUDAH Isaiah 1:1-18

Monday: ISAIAH'S COMMISSION Isaiah 6:1-13

Tuesday: CHRIST—ISRAEL'S HOPE Isaiah 7:10-16; 9:1-21

Wednesday: THE COMING KINGDOM Isaiah 11:1-16

Thursday: A GREAT GOD Isaiah 40:1-31

Friday: CHRIST OUR SUBSTITUTE Isaiah 53:1-12

Saturday: A GLORIOUS SALVATION Isaiah 55:1-13

Chapter 19

LET'S LOOK AT JEREMIAH
and LAMENTATIONS

PORTRAYS JESUS CHRIST,
THE RIGHTEOUS BRANCH

CALL AND COMMISSION (Read Jeremiah 1)

This unique tragedy unfolds in the little village of
Anathoth. The chief actor is a young man named
Jeremiah, ordained before his birth to be a prophet.
(See Jer. 1:5.)

Every man's career is written by God, but it seems
that, to some, God's purpose for their life is only seen
at the end of life, while others are assured from the

very first that God had selected them for a special work. Jeremiah was one of those to whom the will of God was a career.

We hear Jeremiah speak as the scene opens, *Ah, Lord GOD! behold, I cannot speak: for I am a child* [like a young man] (Jer. 1:6). He shrinks from the task God gave him and begs to be excused.

Let us know that a prophet is simply God's messenger-boy delivering not his own ideas, but conveying to the last detail God's thoughts. God had called Jeremiah to be a prophet and the young man is only too conscious of his inexperience, and he almost makes "the great refusal." But God said, *Say not, I am* [still] *a child: for thou shalt go to all that I shall send thee, and whatsoever I command thee thou shalt speak. Be not afraid of their faces: for I am with thee to deliver thee* (Jer. 1:7-8). He made the young Jeremiah conscious of a divine call. The work to which he was commissioned was not his own.

Remember, the path of duty is the path of safety! While Jeremiah is pondering, we hear a voice again saying, *Behold, I have put my words in thy mouth* (Jer. 1:9). No longer could he complain of inability to speak. God promises to put the message into the mouth of His prophets. (See what Christ said to His disciples in Matthew 10:20.) Then the voice added, *See, I have this day set thee over the nations and over the kingdoms, to root out, and to pull down, and . . . to build, and to plant* (Jer. 1:10).

We see from these words that God appointed Jeremiah as the head of the Department of Architecture and Agriculture. Yes, and He gave him the power to act. What God asks us to do, He fits us for, and what He fits us for, He asks us to do! That was quite a position for just a poor country preacher.

Jeremiah's commission was worldwide, including not

only his own country, but all nations and kingdoms of Egypt, Ammon, Moab, Tyre and Sidon. His commission was to root out the idolatry and pride, but he must finally "build and plant." Jeremiah was to go only to those to whom the Lord sent him. And he was to say only what the Lord commanded him to say. This must be true of us also if we are to be true workers together with God.

God told Jeremiah, *Be not afraid of their faces: for I am with thee to deliver thee* (Jer. 1:8). He was not a public speaker, and he shrank from bearing such an unwelcome message to the people. How often he must have thought of that promise of God when he was hailed before princes and rulers. We like to carry good news but to bear bad news is always hard. We are afraid of the faces of people. When they register pleasure, we feel safe. When they show disgust, we melt.

The LORD put forth his hand (Jer. 1:9). Compare this story of Jeremiah's call with that of Isaiah's. (Isaiah 6:7) Paul says that prophecy is a spiritual gift. (I Cor. 14:1) The touch of God's hand was a tangible pledge for Jeremiah that God was with him. He could not get away from it. God put His hand on Saul on the way to Damascus. He has put His hand on thousands and hundreds of thousands ever since. Christ said, *Ye have not chosen me, but I have chosen you, and ordained you, that ye should go and bring forth fruit . . .* (John 15:16).

BEFORE THE FALL OF JERUSALEM
(Read Jeremiah 2–39)

In the early years of his ministry, during the reign of Josiah, Jeremiah's message, for the most part, was a warning to Judah and a call to her to repent. (Read Jer. 3:6,12,13,22,23.) He spared nothing in exposing the moral rottenness of the people. (Read Jer. 7:1-26.) He warned them of coming judgments if they would not return to God. He especially told them of the danger from the north. (Jer. 4:6) He said that the avengers would come like a raging lion from the thickets. They would sweep over the land with chariots like the whirlwind and with horses swifter than eagles, spreading terror before them and leaving ruin in their wake. (Jer. 4:7,13)

It is probable that for some time after his call Jeremiah continued to live in Anathoth. But before long he was compelled to leave his home and move to Jerusalem, for the men of his home town had made a conspiracy to put him to death. (Jer. 11:18-23) The disloyalty of his neighbors, and especially his own relatives, came as a painful shock to the unsuspecting prophet. But Jehovah told him that this was only the beginning of his troubles and it was a time of preparation for still greater trials in the days to come. (Jer. 12:5,6) Jeremiah's chief enemies were the priests and prophets. (Jer. 26:7,8) It was the same in our Lord's case, and it is often the same today. You remember that the Pharisees and Sadducees were always taking counsel concerning how they might kill Jesus. Jesus tells us that today if we live godly lives we will suffer persecution. Many men hate God and they will hate His children.

King Josiah was succeeded by his son Jehoahaz. Jehoahaz was deposed by Necho and carried off in chains to Egypt, where he died. Necho appointed Jehoiakim to be ruler. It was then that Jeremiah first mentioned the seventy year's captivity. (Jer. 25:1-14) God told them just how long the Jews must remain in exile. (Read Daniel 9:2.)

Jeremiah did not hesitate to denounce even the king in his shameless wrong-doing. In Jeremiah 22:13-19 we see him verbally putting Jehoiakim in stocks and then releasing the lash of a righteous scorn, predicting that he would die without being mourned, and would be buried with the burial of an ass!

Standing in the temple, Jeremiah told the people that the temple would be destroyed and Jerusalem itself would become a desolation. Jeremiah's hearers were shocked. (See Jer. 26:7-9.) They called his words blasphemy.

Jeremiah was charged with being unpatriotic. The cry then would have been "Un-Judaistic!" as today it is "Un-American!" For his opponents it was "My country, right or wrong." For Jeremiah it was, "God's will in my country." (See Jer. 26:12-15.) Abraham Lincoln said that it isn't a question of whether God is on our side; it is rather whether we are on God's side. God said to Jeremiah, *Be not afraid . . . for I am with thee* (Jer. 1:8). We may have to endure loneliness and ridicule for Christ's sake, but His promise is sufficient.

This "I am with thee" was the secret of Paul's life. (See Acts 18:10; 27:23.) It is great to have Him with you. We have found out in recent years that the sense of God's presence was the secret of the strength of Washington, Lincoln, and Lee in the dark hours that came to them.

We next see the prophet in a dimly lighted dungeon. What has happened? The rulers had bound him so they would no longer be troubled by the word of the Lord. But the Lord told Jeremiah to write the words down. This, his loyal friend Baruch did. He wrote the words on the roll as the prophet spoke them. *And Jeremiah commanded Baruch, saying, I am shut up; I cannot go into the house of the LORD: Therefore go thou, and read in the roll, which thou hast written from my mouth, the words of the LORD in the ears of the people* (Jer. 36:5-6).

The Royal Investigating Committee immediately sent for Baruch and commanded him to read the roll again.

(Jer. 36:14,15) They decided the roll must be brought to the king. *We will surely tell the king of all these words* (Jer. 36:16). Knowing full well the character of this ruler, they advised Jeremiah and Baruch to go into hiding before the roll was read in the royal presence. (36:19)

In the winter palace of Jehoiakim, surrounded by all the luxury of an Eastern court, the king sat before his hearth. Jehudi read the roll of Jeremiah. All listened intently. When a portion of the roll had been read Jehoiakim could stand no more. With penknife and angry hands the roll was cut to pieces and thrown into the fire. The very act of Jehoiakim seemed to symbolize the doom of the city, the temple, and all the people of Judah. They had heard God's Word and had rejected it. (See Jeremiah 36:20-26.)

How many, like the atheist Voltaire, have taken the penknife of their intellect and have cut to pieces God's Word. They think by destroying the Bible they can do away with its power. Men try to throw into the fire the word of salvation, but remember *the word of the Lord endureth forever* and by it we shall be judged. (I Peter 1:25; John 12:48.)

Of course Jeremiah and Baruch were ordered to be seized but God had "hid them." (Jer. 36:26) How often God does this for His children. He hides us under His wings, and in the hollow of His hand far from harm.

Now the Lord commanded Jeremiah to take another roll, and to write *all the words of the book* (Jer. 36:32).

Jeremiah stood in the temple gate and spoke boldly for God. He warned Judah of God's inevitable judgment of sin. But he always made an appeal to turn back to God and receive forgiveness.

If we have been thrilled by the exploits of a thousand heroes of wars; by the daring men who face almost certain death, we must give Jeremiah a place even with these, for he, too, on innumerable occasions, dared face kings, dungeons or death, fearlessly and faithfully proclaiming *the word of the LORD which came to Jeremiah* (Jer. 36:27).

Jeremiah's was a moral battle, and a moral battle is harder to fight and keep fighting. Many a fellow who could march into the face of a machine gun has fallen before the pop-gun of ridicule. Peter whipped out his sword in the face of the mob in the garden, and cut off an ear of one of them, but just a few hours later he went down into awful defeat before the taunts of a servant maid.

AFTER THE FALL OF JERUSALEM
(Read Jeremiah 40–52)

In the fourth year of Jehoiakim's reign Nebuchadnezzar invaded Judah, and it was then that Daniel and his companions were carried away to Babylon and Jehoiakim himself was put into chains.

Nebuchadnezzar placed Zedekiah, Jehoiakim's brother, on the throne. Only the poor were left in Jerusalem. Jeremiah likened them to bad, worthless figs, in contrast to those who had gone who were good figs. (See Jer. 24.) The picked men of the nation were carried away. You remember that Daniel afterwards became Prime Minister of Babylon. The men who were left were so weak and degenerate that the prophet could see nothing but doom for Jerusalem.

Jeremiah never ceased urging Judah to submit to Babylon, so much so that his enemies accused him of being a traitor. Besides saving his life, King Nebuchadnezzar of Babylon rewarded his stand and made him an offer of any honor he would accept. (See Jer. 39:11, 12.)

At the same time Jeremiah was crying out against

Babylon for her heinous crime in destroying God's children, he told them that Babylon would be demolished and would be in ruins forever. This is literally true of this wonder city of the ancient world. Read again Isaiah 13:17-22 along with Jer. 51:37-43.

By the time of Christ, Babylon's power had gone and in the first century A.D. it was in ruins. Its bricks have been used in building Baghdad and repairing canals. For centuries it has lain in heaps of desolate mounds. Only beasts of the desert inhabit it. This is a remarkable fulfillment of prophecy. When the writer recently stood and looked over its ruins, it was hard to believe that once this was a city of wonder and beauty, filled with luxury and gross extravagance, unsurpassed in the history of the world, but today it is only a heap of fallen bricks.

In 606 B.C. the first deportation of the Jews to Babylon occurred. It was this year that Jeremiah was ordered to write the predictions he had made and to have them read to the people.

These predictions are scattered throughout chapters 24–49 and concern the future of the Jews, the Babylonian captivity, and the coming Messiah.

In the days when David's throne was tottering and Judah was going into captivity the prophet announced the coming Christ, King of the house of David, a righteous Branch. *In his days Judah shall be saved, and Israel shall dwell safely: and this is His name whereby He shall be called, THE LORD OUR RIGHTEOUSNESS* (Jeremiah 23:6).

Judah's future redemption through Christ is given in chapters 30; 31. The Jews may be scattered today but God will bring them back. (Jer. 30:10,11; 31:10)

Jeremiah 23 is dear to the Jews, God's chosen people, and dear to the heart of God. It tells of the future of Judah, redeemed through the work of their

Messiah, Jesus, the Good Shepherd (vs. 1,3) He will gather His sheep from every corner of the earth and they will return to their own country, the Promised Land. This will take place when the King shall come and sit upon the throne of David. (v. 5)

Finally those left in Jerusalem all fled to Egypt in spite of God's warning against it. (See Jer. 43.) They asked Jeremiah to pray for guidance and when it was given they refused to obey it. The prophet and Baruch were compelled to accompany them. Even in Egypt we find the prophet carrying out his commission. He prophesies the conquest of Egypt by Nebuchadnezzar. (See Jer. 43:8-13.) The Jews refused to listen to his warning, and went on worshiping other gods. Jeremiah told them that the judgment of God would fall. (See Jer. 44:26-28.)

This is the last we hear of Jeremiah. How long he lived in Egypt afterwards we know not. Other prophets had at least occasional successes to cheer their hearts in the midst of difficulties, but Jeremiah seemed to be fighting a losing battle to the very end. Disaster, failure and hostility were rewards for his work. He preached to deaf ears and seemed to reap only hate in return for his love for his people. In life he seemed to accomplish little. He was brokenhearted. But God has given us a record that makes him one of the greatest of all the prophets.

THE BOOK OF LAMENTATIONS

Here is another of the Bible's exquisite books of poetry. It is commonly attributed to Jeremiah. Five beautiful, distinct poems are bound together in the book. It is not all sorrow. Above the clouds of the poet's weeping over the sins of his people, God's sun is shining. In Lamentations 3:22-27 the light breaks through to throw a shining rainbow across the murky sky. God's grace always shines above the clouds of sin, (see Romans 5:20), and it will always shine in the heart which is trusting in God through faith in the Lord Jesus Christ who gives *beauty for ashes, the oil of joy for mourning, and the garment of praise for the spirit of heaviness* (Isaiah 61:3).

HISTORY WHEN JEREMIAH PREACHED

Two years before Josiah's death an Egyptian squadron completed a circumnavigation of Africa. A canal was begun to join the Nile and the Red Sea.

Solon, the great law maker, was active at Athens about 594 B.C.

Babylonian arts and sciences were at their zenith, especially astronomy.

Thales of Miletus is said to have predicted an eclipse of the sun in 585 B.C.

QUIZ OF JEREMIAH

Be familiar with Jeremiah's call from God to his life work given in his own words in Jeremiah 1. He was to devote his life to warning Judah of her sins.

What today is threatening Christian democracy in your community? Is drinking? Lawlessness? Divorce? Race prejudice? Lack of church attendance? No Sunday observance? Lax moral and social life? Lack of Christian principles in government?

What is the condition of America today in comparison to the days of the Puritans? See your newspaper, magazines and TV. Listen to the radio. Is America growing in spiritual power? What proof have you for your answer?

What does God do when a nation forgets Him? Is America in danger? What did Jesus say in His parable of the building upon sand? (Matthew 7:24-27)

Are there prophets today warning us of our condition?

Jeremiah suggested a change of heart was necessary. (31:33) Must the nations of the world have a change of heart? Locate Assyria on your map and see the relation of this powerful nation to Judah.

Minimum Daily Requirements / Spiritual Vitamins

Sunday: JEREMIAH WARNS JUDAH Jer. 1:1-10; 2:1-13; 3:12,22,23; 4:14-19; 6:1-30

Monday: A REBUKE Jer. 7:1-15; 9:1-16; 17:5-18

Tuesday: THE POTTER Jeremiah 18:1-17

Wednesday: THE FAITHLESS SHEPHERDS Jeremiah 23:1-40

Thursday: REPENTANCE AND RESTORATION Jeremiah 24; 25

Friday: ISRAEL'S LAST DAYS Jeremiah 30:18–31:40

Saturday: THE OVERTHROW OF JUDAH Jeremiah 52:1-34 COMFORT TO THE SORROWING Lamentations 1–5

Chapter 20

LET'S LOOK AT EZEKIEL

EZEKIEL PORTRAYS JESUS CHRIST,
THE SON OF MAN

Jeremiah, the great prophet whom we have just finished studying, was the last of the prophets in Jerusalem before the exile. His ministry was still going on when the end came. Recall the story. The young prophet Ezekiel was already at work among the exiles in Babylon. God had prepared a witness to the people in their captivity. God needed a voice to warn the people and to remind them of the reason why all these calamities had befallen them. For twenty-two years Ezekiel dealt with the discouraged captives to whom God had sent him.

The word of the LORD came unto me (Ezekiel 24:15). This phrase occurs forty-nine times in Ezekiel.

God's greatest communications can only be made by his servants whose own hearts have been broken. The instrument in God's hands must himself be ready to share in suffering with others. Jesus' body was broken for us.

A QUICK PANORAMA OF EZEKIEL

The pivot of the book is the destruction of Jerusalem.

I. PRE-SIEGE ....(1–24)

Ezekiel began six years before the destruction of Jerusalem with his prophecies and kept predicting its certainty until it occurred.

II. SIEGE ....(25–32)

After that his prophecies deal with Judah's enemies and the overthrow of these heathen nations.

III. POST-SIEGE ....(33–48)

Finally the restoration and re-establishment of Judah is pictured.

Ezekiel is for the Jew today. It tells God's chosen people that God will fulfill His sure promises. Their land, their city, their temple will be restored to them. It reveals God's plan for them.

Ezekiel is for the Christian today. It is a book of the times, for God's time is always revealed by His dealing with the Jew. When Israel begins to return to her land then divine history is being made. When the Jew moves, we know God is getting ready to act. Keep your eye on the plans and accomplishments of the national movements. These groups are preparing "the land" for their people, the Jews, but unknowingly they are setting the stage for the coming King.

The kingdom of Israel had been in Assyrian captivity one hundred years when God brought judgment upon the southern kingdom of Judah. Nebuchadnezzar had come to Jerusalem and carried away ten thousand of the chief men of the southern kingdom and some of the royal seed including Daniel and Ezekiel. (See II Chron. 36:6,7; Dan. 1:1-3; II Kings 24:14-16.) He was finally forced to devastate Jerusalem because the city persisted in allying herself with Egypt. It was a tragic hour for Jerusalem when her walls were laid flat, her houses burned, the temple destroyed and her people dragged away as captives.

The Jews presented a pitiable picture,—no temple, national life gone, little opportunity for business. To such an audience Ezekiel devoted the best years of his life in the beautiful city of Babylon.

Ezekiel used the visual method of preaching all his own. He used symbols, as in the mimic siege of Jerusalem (Ezek. 4), visions (Ezek. 8), parables (Ezek. 17), poems (Ezek. 19), proverbs (Ezek. 12:22,23; 18:2), and prophecies (Ezek. 6; 20; 40-48).

The "glory of God" seems to be the key phrase of Ezekiel. It occurs twelve times in the first eleven chapters. We see "the glory of the Lord" gradually grieved away from the inner sanctuary by the sin of idolatry, and the brightness fills the court. Then it departed to the threshold and rested over the cherubim. As the cherubim rose from the earth, the glory of the Lord abode above their pinions and mounted with them, forsaking the city and moving to the hills. (Ezek. 10)

Young Christians, this is just what can happen to us. We can grieve the Holy Spirit and resist Him until He leaves us and our heart becomes like a ruined temple bereft of its glory.

The same is true of the church of Christ. The glory of the Lord left the house of the Lord because of the sins of God's people. It is also true of individual Christian experience. God's blessing returns to His people when His people return to Him.

Perhaps God is speaking to us as He spoke to Ezekiel— *Thou are not sent to a people of a strange speech and of an hard language, but to the house of Israel . . . go,*

197

get thee to them of the captivity, unto the children of thy people, and speak unto them (Ezekiel 3:5,11). It was difficult to speak to false prophets, shepherds and princes of his own people, but it was God's command.

VISIONS OF EZEKIEL

Ezekiel is a prophet of visions. The key text of the book shows this: "As I was among the captives . . . the heavens were opened, and I saw visions of God" (Ezekiel 1:1). It is urgent that you scan all these visions before you enter into further detailed study.

PREDICTIONS BEFORE THE SIEGE OF JERUSALEM — AGAINST JUDAH (Read Ezekiel 1–24)

Like the prophets generally, Ezekiel entered upon his ministry only after he had a vision and a call from God. Read of Jeremiah's call in Jer. 1:4-10. Turn to Isaiah 6 and review Isaiah's commission.

Ezekiel gives us a very dramatic picture of his vision and call to service. God bids the prostrate prophet rise and accept his commission for service. God wants more than inactive submission. He wants loving service. God calls Ezekiel "son of man." One hundred times this phrase is used. Ezekiel is called to declare the message of God—a message of doom to the people. (Read Ezek. 2:1-10.) This doom is justified by their rebellion. Ezekiel had every temptation to "rebel" but he went without flinching to speak the Word.

The Almighty ordered Ezekiel to "eat the roll" and then go forth as God's prophet. He returned to the captives by the Chebar canal in bitterness of spirit. For seven days he remained silent.

At the end of the week he received another message from God. This time it was more explicit. He was called

to be a watchman. *I have made thee a watchman . . .
give them warning from me . . . and thou givest him
not warning . . . his blood will I require at thine hand.
Yet if thou warn the wicked . . . thou hast delivered thy
soul* (Ezek. 3:17-19).

God places a great responsibility on His watchmen.
How can we be so careless in the light of such words as
these? How can we go to sleep and fail to warn others
of their sins? Let us answer this challenge and heed this
warning.

SYMBOLS OF COMING DOOM OF JERUSALEM

THE SIEGE OF JERUSALEM.................Ezek. 4:1-3
Ezekiel, as a prophet, preached not by word but by symbol.
(See Ezek. 3:22-27.) He attracted attention and drove home
his message by cutting his hair and beard with a sword,
drawing pictures of the city's fall, digging a tunnel under
the wall and dragging his possessions through after him
while the people gathered around him in astonishment.
THE EXILE—ITS DURATION.................Ezek. 4:4-8
This section is curious. Remember Ezekiel was a sign. He
lay upon his side to symbolize the years of punishment
the Jews were to suffer in exile—a day for a year.
THE HARDSHIPS OF THE EXILES.............Ezek. 4:9-17
The horrors of famine due to siege are symbolized here
by the prophet's food and drink, carefully measured out—
about one-half pound of food a day and a pint of water.
The food according to Hebrew law was unclean.
THE FATE OF THE BESIEGED................Ezek. 5:1-17
This last symbol is the most terrible of all. It suggests
the completeness of the destruction. Ezekiel is commanded
to take a sharp sword and use it like a razor on his head
and beard. This is how clean the city will be swept of its
population.
God says, *Ye shall know that I am Jehovah.*
All of these visions and symbols reveal the method of
Ezekiel's prophecy. This is the method used in Daniel and
Revelation.

A physician told that his proudest moment was when, through the failure of an assistant, he was asked by a great surgeon to aid him in his work. He helped to save a life. Spurgeon, in telling the story, says "I realized that God could save the world without me, but when He told me that I might help Him, I praised Him for the privilege and honor."

As a watchman Ezekiel warned individual men of the coming catastrophe which he so clearly saw. It was not enough to warn the crowd. He dealt with individuals, good and bad, who composed the crowd and told them to turn from their evil ways.

God impressed Ezekiel with individual responsiblity. Each one must repent. Each one must hear the Word. How true this is today of every person. Each one must accept Christ for himself. No one can do it for another. *But as many as received him, to them gave he power to become the sons of God, even to them that believe on his name* (John 1:12). (See John 3:16; 5:24; 3:36.)

PREDICTIONS DURING THE SIEGE OF JERUSALEM — JUDGMENT AGAINST JUDAH'S ENEMIES
(Read Ezekiel 25–32)

Ezekiel's gloomy predictions were completed. (Ezek. 1-24) With the news of the fall of Jerusalem he immediately began to prophesy about the future restoration of Israel. God often reveals a bright picture of Israel's future against the back drop of divine judgment. (See Ezek. 33–48.) But before Israel was restored to her land those who were her enemies had to be put out of the way. So at this point we hear of the future doom of these foreign powers. God pronounced His judgment upon Ammon, Moab, Tyre, Sidon and Egypt for their sins against Israel.

PREDICTIONS AFTER THE SIEGE OF JERUSALEM — JUDAH'S RESTORATION (Read Ezekiel 33–48)

Here in the Old Testament, while the Jews were in what seemed hopeless captivity, God declares constantly that He will restore the Jews to their own land, set up the throne and the kingdom of David through David's greater Son. With His reign will come such earthly and spiritual blessings as have not been known since the world began. This is the golden truth about the golden age which is coming to pass here on this earth. (Read Ezek. 34:22-31.)

Gabriel's prophecy at Jesus' birth in Luke 1:30-33 will be literally fulfilled through David's Son, the Lord Jesus Christ. This promise of a Messianic King and Kingdom must be carefully distinguished from our Lord's spiritual rule over hearts and lives. The words of Gabriel to Mary still wait complete, literal fulfillment. (See Ezek. 34:23, 24; 37:24; I Kings 14:8; Jer. 30:9.)

The appearance of the Messiah will usher in a glorious future. God will make a convenant of peace. (Read Lev. 26:6; Jer. 31:31; Ezek. 37:26.) Wonderful blessings are promised to His people. They will be assured of absolute protection from heathen nations ("evil beasts") because they are possessed by none other than God Himself. (See Ezek. 34:31.)

When the Jew speaks of "The Land," he has in mind only one spot—Palestine, Scripture's "Promised Land." It is here that they shall again find themselves nationally. They will return to the worship of Jehovah, and here their Messiah, the returned Christ, shall rule. As portrayed in Ezekiel, it is a place promised to scattered and wandering Israel. To this "restoration" great sections of the Old Testament are devoted. Ezekiel key-notes this in chapter 36:33-35: *Wastes shall be builded . . . land shall be tilled . . . desolate is become like the garden of Eden . . . cities are become fenced . . .*

Today orange groves, grain-fields, industrial plants, population centers all witness to the increasing urge for God's chosen people to return to their beloved homeland in fulfillment of prophecy. The places thought desolate are Eden-like already. (Ezek. 36:8,9,11) Control by the Turk, *worst of the heathen* (7:24), has kept the Jew from inhabiting the land. Omar's Mosque stands on a spot sacred to Jews, the site of the Temple of Solomon. This, too, was foretold in 36:2: *The enemy hath said . . . even the ancient high places are ours in possession.*

National life has been a "valley of dry bones" experience. Jews have been buried in the nations of the world. But Scripture promises that Jerusalem will once again be the world-center. (Ezek. 5:5; Isa. 2:2) So prominent will it become that world hatred and jealousy will be aroused, culminating in Armageddon's fateful battle. (Ezek. 38)

QUIZ OF EZEKIEL

What impresses you most about this prophet? What was his message to Israel? to Judah? What was his message before exile? after exile? How is Christ portrayed by this prophet?

Ezekiel's prophecy is practical for nations and for the church. Israel's captivity was the result of sin. Sin is a reproach to any people. Do you think America's troubles are the results of America's leaving God out? In what ways has she done this? (See Proverbs 14:34.)

Do you grieve the Spirit of God in your life?

1. By not taking time to read the Word.
2. By forgetting to pray.
3. By offering your life as an unclean channel.
4. By allowing idols and self to have the central position.

Remember your body is the temple of the Holy Spirit. Does His presence glow in your life?

Ezekiel was sent to his own people. Do you think it is sometimes easier to go as a missionary to China than to speak to the members of your own family or your own friends? Why?

Minimum Daily Requirements / Spiritual Vitamins

Sunday: THE PROPHET'S CALL Ezekiel 2:1–3:9

Monday: THE PROPHET A WATCHMAN Ezekiel 3:10-27

Tuesday: ISRAEL SHALL BE SAVED Ezekiel 11:14-21; 28:25,26

Wednesday: ISRAEL'S SINS Ezekiel 22:3-31

Thursday: ISRAEL'S FUTURE Ezekiel 34:1-31

Friday: ISRAEL'S RESTORATION Ezekiel 36:1-38

Saturday: VISION OF THE DRY BONES Ezekiel 37:1-14

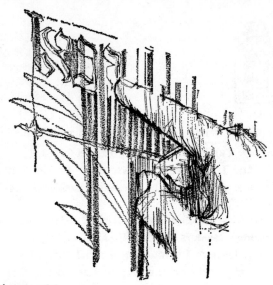

Chapter 21

LET'S LOOK AT DANIEL

DANIEL PORTRAYS JESUS CHRIST,
THE SMITING STONE

Daniel gives us the history of the Gentile powers from Babylon to the end. These prophecies are considered among the most remarkable in the whole Scriptures.

The Book of Daniel is divided into two great sections: Narratives (Dan. 1–6) and Visions (Dan. 7–12).

REIGN OF NEBUCHADNEZZAR (Read Daniel 1–4)

Children in whom was no blemish, but well favoured, and skilful in all wisdom, and cunning in knowledge, and understanding science, and such as had ability in them (Dan. 1:4)—these are some of the men with whom this book deals.

Chief among these princely young men was the incomparable Daniel. He stands in God's Word as the man who dared to keep a clean heart and body (Dan. 1:8), and the man therefore whom God chose to give His message to the Gentile nations of the world. A large part of this book is concerned with the thrilling personal life of this peerless captive prince.

Daniel was in the palace at Babylon at the same time that Ezekiel was toiling in a slave gang. If Daniel's was the easier life in many of its material aspects, it may also be considered the more perilous.

Daniel's whole life from the time of his captivity at the age of sixteen was spent in the great and glamorous city of Babylon. He spent sixty-nine years in a vile court. There he lived a life without blame and well favored. Ezekiel refers to him as a model of righteousness in Ezek. 14:14-20; 28:3.

Although Daniel was a captive he rose to be Prime Minister of Babylon. The wonderful thing is that he always remained true to Jehovah God. We see another striking example in Joseph, of how God raised a young man from the dungeon to the court of Egypt.

Daniel was also great in heaven. God broke the silence of the skies twice to cry out *O Daniel, a man greatly beloved . . . O man greatly beloved* (Dan. 10:11,19). Furthermore, no position, no matter how difficult, found him without trust in God. God is able, in all temptations, to keep us from falling (Jude 24), unless we have deliberately placed ourselves, with Peter, at the fire of the enemy.

Many of the Jews who had been carried into captivity had taken on the loose morals and high life and religion of Babylon. The youth had forgotten, but Daniel and his friends kept themselves apart from the evil of that court in which they lived. They were true to God in a day when everything was against them. As favored ones, they had been given many delicacies of the king's table. They were to be trained in state affairs and equipped for high positions. It was hard indeed to refuse the king's meat and ask for a simpler fare. The king's meat had probably been offered in sacrifice to idols, and the flesh would have been killed with the blood which was unclean. (See Ex. 34:15, I Cor. 10:20; Lev. 3:17; 7:26.) It would look as if these young men had no choice in the matter. Many of us would have argued that way. Remember, we ought always to obey God rather than men.

God gave them favor in the eyes of their companions. There was nothing priggish about Daniel. He was well thought of by his friends. Notice how loyal his companions were to him. This is a fine trait. Success did not turn Daniel's head. He was a man to whom, early in his career, men turned.

We are told that "God gave them knowledge and skill in all learning and wisdom: and Daniel had understanding in all visions and dreams." This was God's reward.

Daniel reveals the power of God and His universal sovereignty. God's power is contrasted with world-power.

Nebuchadnezzar dreamed a dream. This dream and the interpretation teaches us some very interesting things about the history of the world from that time till the "end of this age." This period the Bible calls "the times of the Gentiles" because God has put aside His own people, the Jews, for a time and has passed over world government to the Gentiles.

God revealed His plan of the future to a heathen monarch in a dream. (Read Dan. 2:29.) After Nebuchadnezzar had dreamed, he forgot! But it worried him. No one could tell him his dream but one who knew "the God of heaven," so Nebuchadnezzar sought out Daniel to interpret his dream.

Daniel called his prayer partners (Dan. 2:17) and they presented their problem before God. *Then was the secret revealed unto Daniel in a night vision.* (Dan. 2:19). God never disappoints faith. Daniel knew no other way than the way of prayer.

Picture a great image. The head is of gold, its breast and arms of silver, the belly and thighs of brass, and its legs of iron, with its feet and toes of iron and clay. Then we see a Stone cut out without hands smiting the image and breaking it to pieces; and the Stone became a great mountain and filled the whole earth. This Stone was no other than Jesus Christ, bringing to an end all the other kingdoms. Christ will come and set up a kingdom which will last forever. (Read Dan. 2:44, 45.)

Notice that the metals in the image deteriorate in value—gold, silver, brass and iron. This reveals the weakening in the power of each succeeding empire. Finally we will find a condition of iron mixed with brittle clay, suggesting attempted unions between a democratic and an imperialistic form of government. Name the forms of government that exist today. Do these resemble the toes of clay "brittle" and not holding together?

Many ask, "When will this Stone fall?" We know not the day nor hour, but the King is coming with power and great glory with all His holy angels to establish His kingdom.

Remember at the time Nebuchadnezzar dreamed his dream the Persian kingdom did not exist. It was merely a Babylonian satrapy. It would have seemed impossible that a strong Grecian empire would rise. Only wandering tribes inhabited the Hellenic states. The city of Rome was only a little town on the banks of the Tiber. Yet God told Daniel what would come to pass.

The great King Nebuchadnezzar fell on his face and worshiped Daniel, and declared that his God was the God of all gods. But we find as we go on in the story that this wonderful revelation of God had little real effect upon Nebuchadnezzar. It did not bring him to his knees before God.

As the curtain is pulled back again we face a very tense moment. (Dan. 3) Nebuchadnezzar had set up a golden image on the plain of Dura and had commanded all peoples to fall down and worship it. If any refused, he would be cast into a fiery furnace.

But there were three in the throng that refused to obey the king. Yes, here they are again, after twenty years, Shadrach, Meshach and Abednego. Spies reported their disobedience. These three knew what God had said. *Thou shalt not make unto thee any graven image . . . Thou shalt not bow down thyself to them* (Ex. 20:4,5). They were fearless in the presence of this despot.

The story of the fiery furnace is a familiar one. What was the wonderful thing about that scene? Yes, the Son of God was with them. What effect did this have on Nebuchadnezzar? He was filled with great admiration for the miraculous power of the God of these men. Again he does not bow to worship God in humility. He calls Jehovah "their God." Remember God wants us to say, "My Lord, and My God." Christ said, "When ye pray, say, our Father." This scene demonstrated, in a most dramatic way, before the dignitaries of the far-flung empire, the power of the Most High God. The erecting of an image will be repeated by the beast, the Antichrist last head of Gentile world-dominion. (Read Rev. 13:11-15; 19:20.)

REIGN OF BELSHAZZAR (Read Daniel 5-8)

Here we see a great banquet hall with a thousand lords sitting about the tables. It was "ladies' night." All the king's sweethearts were there beside the thousand lords. Often the presence of ladies seems to inspire a man to do something spectacular. So as an extra feature, Belshazzar adorned the table with sacred golden and silver vessels which his grandfather Nebuchadnezzar had stripped from the temple of Jerusalem. He showed just how little he regarded the God of Israel. Belshazzar was the last prince of Babylon. He was drinking wine to the idols in these sacred vessels.

God showed His power in the awful handwriting on the wall. Daniel was called in to explain the meaning. The prophet fearlessly condemned this foolish and sensual young king. Read the details of the divine interruption in Daniel 5.

A bad reign came to a sudden end. *In that night was Belshazzar the king of the Chaldeans slain.* We are not told how, but we find from Xenophon and Herodotus and Berosus the strange story of the fall of the great city. Inscriptions on Babylonian tablets tell how the phenomenal overthrow of Belshazzar was accomplished. To quote from the discoverer of these tablets: "Cyrus diverted the Euphrates into a new channel, and, guided by two deserters, marched by the dry river bed into the city while the Babylonians were carousing at the annual feast of the gods."

During the first year of Belshazzar's reign, Daniel had a vision of four wild beasts, which symbolized the four kingdoms pictured in Nebuchadnezzar's dream. Picturing them as beasts gives us a hint as to the moral character of these empires for they are represented by ferocious wild beasts. How wars reveal the true heart of nations! (Dan. 7)

In Nebuchadnezzar's dream-image we have man's

view of the magnificence of these kingdoms. (Dan. 2) In Daniel's dream we have God's view of the same. See who these four beasts are in Dan. 7:17-23. The first, Babylon, was like a lion with eagle's wings. Persia was the bear, the cruel animal who delights to kill for the sake of killing. The third was a leopard or panther, a beast of prey. His four wings portray swiftness. Here we see the rapid marches of Alexander's army and his insatiable love of conquest. In thirteen short years he had conquered the world. The fourth beast was different from all the rest. He was *dreadful and terrible, and strong exceedingly; and it had great iron teeth.* (Dan 7:7).

This vision of the four beasts covers the same ground as the great image of Daniel 2. Compare them carefully.

REIGN OF DARIUS (Read Daniel 6; 9)

Twenty-three years after the death of Nebuchadnezzar, his great city, Babylon, fell into the hands of the Medes.

Even under these new rulers, Daniel was in a place of power. The jealousy of the other officials was aroused by the preference given to Daniel and a plot to destroy him was quickly formed. *Then the presidents and princes sought to find occasion against Daniel* (Dan 6:4). Of course they tried. He "okayed" all their tax receipts and they soon found that Daniel would not allow any graft. If Daniel didn't let them "get by," how were they going to get along with the high cost of living in Babylon? So Daniel had trouble because he would not stand in with the political crowd.

They used his religion to set their trap, with the very same result as always when men are fools enough to try to trip the Lord's faithful children. (See I Peter 3:12,13; Deut. 9:3.) Remember there is always access to God through Christ. We may speak to Him not just three times a day but whenever we like.

Gladstone was a statesman whose windows were always "open toward Jerusalem." "That Gladstone!" sneered his enemies, just as Daniel's enemies did. See their words *That Daniel!* (Dan. 6:13).

All unconsciously the king was induced to pass the decree solely for Daniel's destruction. Just imagine, if you can, a David, an Alexander, a Caesar, a Peter the Great, a Napoleon, a Queen Victoria, or any other strong ruler letting a cabal of his court trick him into sacrificing a favorite if he did not want to! Signing that law without finding out what was back of it was inexcusable. When he found the trap he had walked into, he should have broken the promise. "A bad promise is better broken than kept."

The envy of these men no doubt was due to Daniel's ability and his Jewish blood. This spirit of "Anti-Semitism" is in fulfillment of God's prophecies that the Jews would be hated. It continues rampant today.

Daniel's conduct in face of danger was quite deliberate. He knew he had to deny his religion or be prepared to die for it. There was nothing different in his actions. He prayed as was his custom. His example would influence the other Jews. By drawing attention to himself, he might reduce the danger for others. Daniel's faith during this ordeal was glorious and just what we would expect from a man ripened in years with God.

The officials knew that the king would not lift a finger against Daniel, so they had to trap the king. What was their bait? Notice the subtle appeal to the king's pride.

The law of the Medes and Persians was unchangeable. (See Esther 1:19; 8:8.) The king saw that he had been deceived, and realizing the injustice of putting

Daniel to death, did his best to avoid carrying out the law.

Contrast the edict of Darius before and after Daniel's deliverance from the den of lions. (Dan. 6:26-27) Over the vast realm a proclamation went, declaring the power and greatness of Daniel's God. This scene closes with Daniel's prospering during the reign of Darius, and also on to the reign of Cyrus.

How could such a busy man as Daniel take so much time for prayer? Martin Luther, when once asked by his friends what his plans for the following day were, said, "Work, work from early until late. In fact, I have so much to do that I shall pray the first three hours."

Daniel was thrown into the den of lions, but he fell into the hands of the living God. The world cannot breed a lion that God cannot tame. Shutting lions' mouths of difficulty and temptation is God's specialty.

Notice that Daniel prayed with thanksgiving. (Read Dan. 6:10; Phil. 4:6,7.) When Daniel found out that the writing was signed, he did not fall down in terror and agony, but he praised God. *Commit thy way unto the LORD; trust also in him; and he shall bring it to pass* (Psalm 37:5).

REIGN OF CYRUS (Read Daniel 10–12)

It was during the reign of Cyrus that the decree was sent out for the captives to return and build the walls of Jerusalem. (Read Ezra 1:2-4.) Daniel, now nearly ninety years old, was too old to return. No doubt he was needed among the exiles in Babylon. Daniel had outlived all the friends and companions of his youth. Now he saw the Jews gathering in the streets of Babylon and the aged man watched the last caravan leave the west gate of the city to return to Jerusalem. Daniel was concerned about his people. We will see how he was comforted in his perplexity. (Dan. 10)

In Daniel 11 we find the vision which concerns the near future of the kingdom in which Daniel was so great a personage. Three kings were yet to come in the Medo-Persian empire. Then Alexander, the mighty king of Greece, would appear. (See Dan. 11:2,3.) His empire would be divided among his four generals as had already been predicted. The course of affairs is followed down to Antiochus Epiphanes, the "little horn" of Dan. 8. His desecration of the sanctuary is again mentioned. (Dan. 12:11)

Beginning with Dan. 11:36 we see the description of the final "little horn" of Dan. 7.

The great tribulation follows. How is it described in Dan. 12:1? This is a time of unparalleled trouble. Our Lord spoke of it in Matt. 24:21. What does He say? Mention is made of two resurrections. (Read Dan. 12:2.) These two will be one thousand years apart. (See Rev. 20:1-6.) The first is the resurrection of the saints, at Christ's coming, to life everlasting. This is followed by one thousand years, called the millennium. Then the resurrection of the wicked to shame everlasting. *Many of them that sleep in the dust of the earth shall awake, some to everlasting life, and some to shame and everlasting contempt* (Dan 12:2). Those now that *turn many to righteousness* are given significant rewards, showing us the necessity of diligence in soul-winning during our wait for Christ's return. (See Dan. 12:3.)

It is a remarkable fact that Sir Isaac Newton, in his work on the prophecies of Daniel and Revelation, said that if they were true it would be necessary that a new mode of traveling should be invented. He added that the knowledge of mankind would be so increased before a certain date that they would be able to travel at the rate of fifty miles an hour.

Voltaire got hold of this and, true to the spirit of the

skeptic of all ages, said, "Now look at the mighty mind of Newton, who discovered gravitation. When he became an old man and got into his dotage, he began to study the Book called the Bible. It seems in order to credit its fabulous nonsense we must believe that the knowledge of mankind will be so increased that we shall be able to travel at the rate of fifty miles an hour. The poor dotard."

The self complacency of the infidel made his friends laugh, but if a skeptic today should get into an airplane, he would have to say, "Newton was a wise philosopher, Voltaire a poor old dotard."

QUIZ OF DANIEL

We found the great test of Daniel came through his appetite. He chose not to touch the king's meat. Today nine out of ten of America's greatest tests of character come through the appetites. How shall we tackle the problem of drink?

Is drinking a problem today? Do youth frequent night clubs and roadhouses? What are the dangers of drink physically, mentally, morally?

Are you influenced by the action of the crowd? Does your ambition to be popular make you cut corners when you know what is right? Can people tell that you are a Christian by your behavior?

Can you tell someone else about Nebuchadnezzar's dream? (Dan. 2) The great feast of Belshazzar? (Dan. 5) Daniel in the lions' den? (Dan. 6)

Describe the great image pictured in Dan. 3.

See the vision of Daniel in chapter 7 and compare it with Nebuchadnezzar's dream in chapter 2.

Master the outline of history given in Dan. 2.

We find race prejudice and minority group feeling in Daniel. How was it revealed?

How is Christ portrayed by Daniel?

TEST YOURSELF—

Daniel was separated from his home. How did he act? How do you behave when you have no supervision?

1. Do you study without coercion?
2. Do you cut corners to be popular?
3. Are you true in your Christian witness?

Daniel kept true to God all through life.

1. Are you faithful in your prayer life?
2. Are you faithful in church attendance?
3. Are you a witness to Christ by life and lip?

Daniel was true in all things.

1. Do you cheat?
2. Do you smoke? Drink?
3. Do you watch your social actions?

Minimum Daily Requirements / Spiritual Vitamins

Sunday: DANIEL THE CAPTIVE Daniel 1;2

Monday: NEBUCHADNEZZAR, THE PROUD KING
Daniel 3;4

Tuesday: BELSHAZZAR'S REIGN Daniel 5; 7; 8

Wednesday: DARIUS' REIGN Daniel 6; 9

Thursday: GOD'S GLORY Daniel 10

Friday: THE CONFLICT OF KINGS Daniel 11

Saturday: DANIEL'S LAST MESSAGE Daniel 12

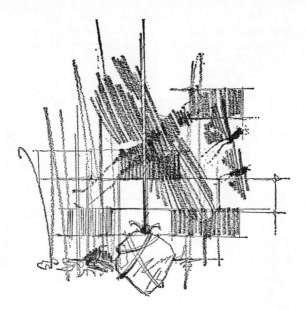

Chapter 22

LET'S LOOK AT HOSEA, JOEL, AMOS

*JESUS CHRIST, HEALER OF THE BACKSLIDER;
RESTORER; HEAVENLY HUSBANDMAN*

With the study of Hosea's prophecy we enter upon twelve books known as the minor prophets. Remember, the difference between the major and minor prophets is not a matter of importance but of the amount of material written.

Hosea was sent to the ten northern tribes called "Israel." He prophesied in the reign of Jeroboam II of Israel. He lived in this northern kingdom when the splendors of Jeroboam's brilliant reign of forty-one years was beginning to fade into the black midnight of Israel's captivity. He prophesied during the eighth century B.C. This was a stirring time in the world's history. Rome and Carthage were both founded during this period. Hosea's contemporaries were Amos, Isaiah and Micah.

ISRAEL'S UNFAITHFULNESS (Read Hosea 1–3)

As the scene opens we see a young man marrying a girl unworthy of him. What was her name? He loved her truly. God told him to do something which would have been very repulsive to him. What was it? (Hosea 1:2,3) It was a severe test. He was to be a sign of Israel.

Just as Hosea was married to an unfaithful bride, Gomer, so God was married to unfaithful Israel. This experience of Hosea helped him to understand God's heart of love as He yearned over wayward Israel to come home to Him.

God frequently uses marriage to symbolize His relation to Israel. *As the bridegroom rejoiceth over the bride, so shall thy God rejoice over thee* (Isaiah 62:5). And, *I am married* [a husband] *unto you* (Jer. 3:14). Israel is Jehovah's bride while the Church is the Lamb's bride. God said of Israel, *I will betroth thee unto me forever* (Hosea 2:19). God had been true to His bride, the Jews. He had loved them, and protected them, and lavished every gift upon them. But they left God and went after other gods. They disobeyed His laws. Like Hosea's wife, they had broken their marriage vows and had fallen into slavery, sin and shame. Israel, like Gomer, had forgotten who had given her past blessings in abundance. (See Hosea 2:8.)

ISRAEL'S NATIONAL SIN (Read Hosea 4–10)

Hosea, whose name means "salvation," was not only a poet laureate to the king, but he was God's voice to the people. They did not care to hear his message to a backslidden nation. (Hosea 14:1) He called their attention to a wretched present. *Without a king, and without a prince, and without a sacrifice, and without an image, and without an ephod, and without teraphim* (Hosea 3:4). He also spoke a glorious future. *Afterward shall the children of Israel return, and seek the LORD their God, and David their king; and shall fear the LORD and his goodness in the latter days* (Hosea 3:5).

This was Israel's condition. They were stiff-necked and rebellious. God cannot do anything with a stiff-necked will.

Do not give God hardened clay models of lives all fashioned after our own will for Him to use, but rather put plastic clay into His hand to mould.

God's Word is a mirror. What is a mirror really for? Is it to see how well you look? No! I believe it is to see the flaws—to see what is wrong so you may correct it. *Hear the Word of the Lord, ye children of Israel: for the LORD hath a controversy with you* (Hosea 4:1).

"Sometimes I think that God has been hard with me, when I forget how hard I have been with God."

ISRAEL'S BLACKLIST OF SIN

"Falsehood" ....Hosea 4: 1
"Licentiousness" ....Hosea 4:11
"Murder" ....Hosea 5: 2
"Robbery" ....Hosea 7: 1
"Oppression" ....Hosea 12: 7

ISRAEL'S HOPE (Read Hosea 11–14)

A picture of Israel's blessings in the future kingdom breaks over this last scene. We get a glimpse into God's heart of love when He, as a father, says, *When Israel was a child, then I loved him, and called my son out of Egypt* (Hosea 11:1).

As God looked over the vast and glittering expanse of empires, He did not choose Israel for His people because they were the greatest or richest of the nations of the world. (Deut. 7:6-8) He rather chose a weak, unattractive slave child to be the object of His love and care and blessings. (Hosea 11:1)

But Israel began to grow persistently disobedient and rebellious. The more the prophets warned them the farther they went away from God. They showed no gratitude to God for all the blessings of their land. In their freedom they forgot God and fell into sin and idolatry and were plunging into captivity. (Hosea 11:2) **Israel finished her training in the slave markets of Assyria and Babylon. (Read Hosea 4:6, 7.)**

We must understand God's attitude toward sin. He says, *The wages of sin is death* (Rom. 6:23). *Be not deceived; God is not mocked: for whatsoever a man soweth, that shall he also reap* (Gal. 6:7).

Read again in Hosea 9:17 to see the condition of the Jew today—*wanderers among the nations.* God will do more than forgive their backslidings; He will cure them and remove the cause.

Read the wonderful words of the Lord to backsliding Israel in Hosea 14:4, *I will heal their backsliding, I will love them freely: for mine anger is turned away from him.* God's great heart is bursting with love, but our sins keep Him from telling us all that is there.

THE BOOK OF JOEL

THE WARNING (Read Joel 1)

Joel is considered to be one of the earliest of all the prophets whose writings have come down to us. He no doubt would have known both Elijah and Elisha in his youth.

The curtain rises on a very dark scene. Appalling

famine, caused by an awful plague of locusts, followed by a prolonged drought, devastates the land. People and flocks were dying.

Graphically Joel describes the plague, calling the old men to confirm the fact that there had never been one like it before. (Joel 1:2) Drunkards felt the effect of it, for the vines had been destroyed. (Joel 1:5) Priests had no meat-offering, nor drink-offering of wine to offer. (Joel 1:9) Cattle and sheep cried in the fields. (Joel 1:20) Joel urged the people to call a fast. (Joel 1:13) Then he continues to describe the plague.

Joel calls the people to consider the cause of the calamity. They must be truly penitent if they wish to be spared further judgment. (Read Joel 2:12-17.) Desperate, they were ready to listen to anyone who could explain their plight. It was a great hour for the preacher, for now, in their extremity, men turn to God.

When we know that God has allowed calamities to come upon us because of our sins, we should repent lest a greater thing come upon us. God was showing Judah that the locusts swarming the land were a figure of the nations who should swarm upon Israel if the people would not return to God. If they would repent, God would pour out His Spirit upon them. God's mercy is shown in every judgment. (Read Joel 2:18-32.)

A young man had been led to Christ through an accident in which his leg was cut off. He used to point to the stump and say, "I love that old leg, for it was that which brought me to God." Often God has to allow misfortune to bring us to ourselves. This has been true of Israel. How sad it is when we do not learn our lesson.

THE PROMISE (Read Joel 2)

The blast of the ram's horn calling an assembly for a great fast opens this scene. (Joel 2:1) Everyone was there—old and young alike. Even brides and bride-grooms on their wedding day attend. (Joel 2:16) The priests came in sackcloth, and bowed to the ground and cried to God within the sanctuary. *Spare the people, O LORD* and to the people, *Rend your heart, and not your garments, and turn unto the LORD your God* (Joel 2:13). It was an event to bring the people back to God.

The locusts had made an Eden into a desolate wilderness. (Joel 2:3) But God said, *I will restore to you the years that the locusts hath eaten* (Joel 2:25). Repentance could bring them again into God's favor. "I will make up to you," are His words.

The prophet assured the people that God would indeed send both temporal mercies and spiritual blessings. (Joel 2:18-32) Yes, and God will send deliverance from the sky! *And it shall come to pass afterward, that I will pour out my spirit upon all flesh; and your sons and your daughters shall prophesy, your old men shall dream dreams, your young men shall see visions: And also upon the servants and upon the handmaids in those days will I pour out my spirit* (Joel 2:28,29). Here is the prophecy of Pentecost. Read the fulfillment of this prophecy in Acts 2. Peter said, *This is that which was spoken by the prophet Joel* (Acts 2:16).

THE FUTURE (Read Joel 3)
JOEL, JUDAH, THE FUTURE

Enemies	Overthrown!	Joel 3:1-15
Jerusalem	Delivered	Joel 3:16-17
Land	Blessed	Joel 3:18
Judah	Restored!	Joel 3:19-21

Only God could have told Joel of the return of the Jews from captivity. Joel not only saw the return from Babylon, but the last regathering of the Jews from among the Gentile nations. He also tells of the judgment of the nations after the battle of Armageddon.

(Joel 3:2-7) (Read Matt. 25:32 and Rev. 19:17-21.) Man's day of decision is over. God's hour of destiny has arrived.

After Israel has been restored and the nations of the earth have been judged (Joel 3:1,2), then will the everlasting kingdom be set up. (Joel 3:20) Once again Palestine, the Land of Promise, will be the center of power and the gathering place of the nations for judgment. Christ will return to establish His rule as Sovereign.

THE BOOK OF AMOS

In Amos we find one of many instances in the Bible of God calling a man when he was occupied in his daily work. (Amos 1:1) God called him, lariat in hand, and sent him forth to lasso his straying people. David was caring for his sheep and Gideon was threshing when they received their commissions.

This raw young herdsman, Amos, had a certain rugged frankness about him that was refreshing. He always hit straight from the shoulder. He didn't fail to tell even King Jeroboam what he should do.

You have heard of the young preacher who was afraid of the influential members in his congregation and this was the way he soothed them, "You must repent, as it were, and be converted, so to speak, or you will be damned, to some extent." Amos never preached like that. God wanted someone to bear His message courageously, and Amos did not fail Him. Israel needed a prophet who would tear the scales from their eyes and let them know the sure consequences of their idolatry. God abhors sin. Sin must be punished. Sinners must suffer.

To every question as to why great empires have fallen, the answer is sin. The secret of a great man's undoing is sin. Let Amos help you see sin in its true light.

If a ship at sea follows a wrong course, what happens? Yes, some sort of trouble, and wreckage in the end. But what of a captain who follows a wrong course knowingly? Something is wrong with his head. No wonder prophets like Amos spoke plainly in warning people about the wrong course of sin.

GOD'S JUDGMENT AGAINST NATIONS
(Read Amos 1–6)

Amos started his preaching to the assembled crowds at Bethel. It was the religious capital of the northern kingdom, Israel. He proclaimed the Lord's judgment upon six neighboring nations—Damascus (Syria), Gaza (Philistia), Tyrus (Phoenicia), Edom, Ammon, and Moab. Then he came nearer home and pronounces judgment against Judah (Amos 2:4), and against Israel itself (Amos 2:6), and finally the whole nation. (Amos 3:12) Amos' approach is clever. We are always willing to hear of our enemy's doom. Our own is harder to swallow, but we are forced to take it.

The punishment of Judah was fulfilled in the destruction of Jerusalem by Nebuchadnezzar. (Amos 2:5)

Amos denounces the sin of Israel more graphically than Hosea. (Chapter 2) He speaks of their careless ease and luxury, their oppression of the poor, the lying and cheating that existed, and worse than all, their hypocrisy in worship. The Lord grieved over His people not heeding His warnings. *Yet have ye not returned unto me, saith the LORD* (Amos 4:6). Then the invitation, "Seek ye Me, and ye shall live." (Amos 5:4)

God always warns before a punishment, yes, and offers a way of escape. God denounces sin, but He offers a remedy for sin. Israel's rejection of repeated

warnings should lead them to prepare for God's judgment. (Amos 5) If Israel had sought the Lord, the "day
of the Lord," spoken of in Amos 5:20, would not have
overtaken them. They did not seek Him and Assyrian
fighters ushered in that day.

VISIONS OF AMOS

VISIONS REGARDING THE FUTURE
(Read Amos 7–9)

Amos, as do most of the prophets, tells us of a bright
future for God's chosen people. The whole land will
once more be a kingdom under the house of David.
(Amos 9:11,12) The tabernacle of David, now torn
down, shall be rebuilt. (Acts 15:16,17) Israel shall be
restored to her land and prosper. A happy people shall
dwell in a happy land.

Always keep in mind that the Jew, today scattered
over the face of the world, is going to be gathered back
to her Land of Promise. National prosperity will again
flourish. Jerusalem shall be the capital of a mighty
kingdom. Converted Israel shall be God's witnesses.
(Amos 9:13-15)

QUIZ OF HOSEA, JOEL AND AMOS

As Hosea, are you faithful to God in your conversation?
In your actions? In your thoughts?
How do you sin?
In your mind? Do you ever doubt God?
In your acts? Do you cheat? Steal time?
By your lips? Are you silent when you should speak?

Why did God choose Israel? Why did God choose you?

How often a young nation in its days of small beginnings and hardships worships God and grows strong in virtue. But when she becomes mighty and rich, she forgets Him. Think of the Puritans coming to America through a long and perilous voyage upon a stormy and little known sea, with the old Book and God in their hearts! The log cabins were always built around the log church. Is God in the center of America now? Have we a right to sing, "God Bless America"?

Acquaint yourself with Joel's promise of Pentecost. Read the fulfillment of this promise in Acts 2.

Study these "Plumbline Proverbs" in Amos in relationship to Israel:

A plumbline always reveals the crooked wall.

National sins mean national punishment.

God's favor never means favoritism, but responsibility.

God does not warn indefinitely before He brings judgment.

A right relationship to God means righteous dealing with others.

Minimum Daily Requirements / Spiritual Vitamins

Sunday: ISRAEL'S WILFUL IGNORANCE Hosea 4

Monday: ISRAEL'S GLORIOUS FUTURE Hosea 3; 14

Tuesday: PUNISHMENT AND BLESSING Joel 2

Wednesday: THE RESTORATION OF ISRAEL Joel 3

Thursday: PERSONAL ADMONITIONS Amos 3:1-7; 4:6-12

Friday: THE PROPHET'S INTERCESSION Amos 7:1-17; 8:1-7

Saturday: FUTURE KINGDOM BLESSINGS Amos 9:1-15

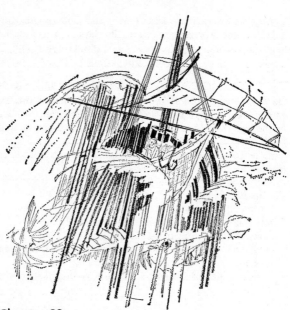

Chapter 23

LET'S LOOK AT OBADIAH, JONAH, MICAH

JESUS CHRIST, OUR SAVIOUR;
OUR RESURRECTION AND LIFE;
WITNESS AGAINST REBELLIOUS NATIONS

Petra was one of the wonders of the world. It was located in the land of Edom over fifty miles south of the Dead Sea. It was perched like an "eagle's nest" amid inaccessible mountain fastnesses. (Obad. 4) Its only approach was through a deep rock cleft more than a mile long with massive cliffs more than seven hundred feet high rising on either side. The city was able to withstand any invasion. We are told that its temples numbered a thousand. They were cut out of the pink rock on the side of the massive cliffs. The dwellings were mostly caves hewn out of the soft red sandstone and placed where you can hardly believe it possible for a human foot to climb. (Obad. 3; 6)

It is here that Esau settled after he had sold his birthright to his brother Jacob. Having driven out the Horites (Gen. 14:5,6), he occupied the whole of the mountain. Sela, or Petra, "Rock," was their capital. Today it is called "the silent city of the forgotten past."

The descendants of Esau (Jacob's brother) were called Edomites. They would go out on raiding expeditions, and then retreat to their impregnable fortress where they kept alive in their hearts a bitter enmity toward the Jews that began with Jacob and Esau.

DOOM OF EDOM (Read Obadiah 1–16)

This book is the shortest in the Old Testament. It contains only twenty-one verses, but it includes two important themes—the *doom* of the proud and rebellious and the *deliverance* of the meek and humble.

Of the prophet who wrote this book we know nothing. His contemporary was Jeremiah. No doubt it was in the awful day when Nebuchadnezzar took Jerusalem and reduced it to a desolate heap. The Edomites had helped the marauders by catching the fleeing Israelites, treating them with cruelty and selling them as slaves. This prophecy was written because of this confederacy against Jerusalem in which Edom took the part of the enemy. (Obad. 7–14)

God had commanded Israel *Thou shalt not abhor an Edomite; for he is thy brother* (Deut. 23:7). But Edom had shown an implacable hatred to Israel.

Because of the pride and cruel hatred of Edom, their utter destruction was decreed. (Obad. 3; 4; 10) Nothing could save the guilty nation. The people were driven from their rocky home five years after the destruction of Jerusalem, when Nebuchadnezzar, passing down the valley of Arabah, which formed the military road to Egypt, crushed the Edomites. They lost their existence as a nation with the capture of Jerusalem by the Romans. *As thou hast done, it shall be done unto thee* (Obad. 15).

DELIVERANCE FOR ZION (Read Obadiah 17–21)

God's chosen people had just been carried into captivity by Nebuchadnezzar; the Holy Land was deserted; and God had told Edom of their doom. Five years later Edom fell before the same Babylon she had helped. She would be as though she had never been— swallowed up forever. This was the prophecy against Edom. But Israel shall rise again from her present fall. She will repossess not only her own land, but also Philistia and Edom. She will finally rejoice in the holy reign of the promised Messiah. God's chosen people, the Jews, shall possess their possessions and among the dearest of them is their Holy Land. Obadiah, as the other prophets, predicts the coming of the day of the Lord and the establishment of Messiah's kingdom.

THE BOOK OF JONAH

Jonah is the *test* book of the Bible. It challenges our faith. Our attitude toward Jonah reveals our attitude toward God and His Word. Is the story of Jonah mere naturalism or super-naturalism? Right here we stand or fail.

"I cannot swallow Jonah," some people say. Who asked you to? God prepared a fish to do that.

Dr. A. C. Dixon used to say, "If God said He had prepared a Waldorf Astoria apartment in the belly of the fish, steam heated and electric lighted, I could easily believe it because I believe God is able to do anything." He is God, the miracle working God! Who are we? Our engineers build submarines and we are not amazed. Cannot God do as well?

Read this short book through. Many stumble over this book. Few know it.

God is in this book. He is taking care of His prophet. Find the statement four times concerning Him, as follows:

GOD PREPARED

A great fish ....Jonah 1:17
A gourd ....Jonah 4:6
A worm ....Jonah 4:7
A sultry east wind ....Jonah 4:8

Jesus Christ, Himself, made the book of Jonah important. When He was asked for a sign to prove His claims, He gave the people the sign of Jonah. (Read Matthew 12:38-40.)

There are two events of great importance in Jonah. One is the great fish swallowing Jonah and the other the possibility of such a large heathen city as Nineveh being converted by an obscure foreign missionary in just a few days. See what Jesus said in Matthew 12:38-42.

AN OBSTINATE PROPHET (Read Jonah 1; 2)

As the scene opens God is speaking to Jonah, a famous statesman in Israel. He is giving him his commission. What is it? (Jonah 1:2)

God is very definite with His orders. He told Jonah to arise and go. But Jonah rose up to flee *unto Tarshish from the presence of the LORD, and went down to Joppa* (Jonah 1:3). He said "No" to God. Why did he flee? Read Jonah 4:2. Jonah knew that Assyria was

Israel's dreaded enemy. Jonah fears that Nineveh may repent and be spared impending doom. If Assyria falls, Jonah's own beloved Israel may escape judgment at Assyria's hands. Jonah has the spirit of a national hero. He decides to sacrifice himself in order to save his people but his heroism is sadly misguided.

Nineveh was one of the greatest cities of the world, situated on the bank of the Tigris, four hundred miles from the Mediterranean. It was the capital of Assyria. (Gen. 10:11,12) The stronghold of the city was about thirty miles long and ten miles wide. It was marvelous in appearance. There were five walls and three moats (canals) surrounding it. The walls were one hundred feet high and allowed four chariots to be driven abreast. There were palaces great and beautiful with the finest of gardens. Fifteen gates guarded by colossal lions and bulls opened into the city. There were seventy halls decorated magnificently in alabaster and sculpture. The temple in the city was in the form of a great pyramid which glittered in the sun. The city was as great in wickedness as it was in wealth and power.

As soon as Jonah fled, God began to act. He *sent out* [or hurled] *a great wind into the sea, and there was a mighty tempest in the sea* . . . (Jonah 1:4). God loved Jonah too much to let him prosper. Failure never relieves us of responsibility to serve.

Read events that took place before the throwing of Jonah into the sea. (Jonah 1:3-15) Jonah was cast into the sea, but he was gripped by the hand of God. (Jonah 1:17) God's way is best. If we don't accept it, He forces strange things upon us.

The story of Jonah 2 tells us how Jonah came to the end of himself. After much praying he confessed that he could do nothing by himself. *Salvation is of the LORD* (Jonah 2:9). Then God could afford to set him at liberty. (Jonah 2:10)

AN OBEDIENT PROPHET (Read Jonah 3; 4)

God gave Jonah another chance to be of service. *And the word of the LORD came unto Jonah the second time.* How foolish he was to make God repeat His call. How foolish not to obey at once!

God said again, *Arise, go unto Nineveh, that great city, and preach unto it the preaching that I bid thee* (Jonah 3:2). God gives us a well defined message. Peter obeyed God and lo, Pentecost! We are like telegraph messengers. We must bear the telegram just as it is to the person to whom it is sent. We cannot change it.

It was not easy for Jonah to go through the streets and cry, *Yet forty days, and Nineveh shall be overthrown* (Jonah 3:4). There was no mercy in his message. There was no tear in the prophet's voice. He was obeying God but his heart was unchanged. (See Jonah 4:1-3.) The common people of Nineveh repented first. Then the nobles followed. This is always true. Revival starts among the people. Think of a city like Chicago repenting and turning to God in one day because of the preaching of a modern prophet. It would be a miracle of the ages. But this is what happened when Jonah preached in his day.

Look at him sulking, as he sits on the hill on the east side of the city under a gourd that God "prepared" for a shade over his head, waiting to see what God would do. (Jonah 4:6)

The book ends abruptly! But we must notice two things in this book. First, Jonah is a type of Christ in his death, burial, and resurrection. *As Jonah was three days and three nights in the whale's belly; so shall the Son of man be three days and three nights in the heart of the earth* (Matt. 12:40). Second, Jonah is also a type of Israel—disobedient to God, swallowed by the nations of the world, who will yet give her up when Christ comes. Then shall Israel be witnesses of God everywhere.

Above all, do not disobey God. Look at the Jew today! He is in a kind of "whale's belly" till he learns his lesson. But the Lord will come to him "a second time" and the Jew will preach and men will hear. We are looking for that day.

> God is GOD; do not resist Him.
> God is GOOD; trust Him, not man.

THE BOOK OF MICAH

Micah was a country preacher who lived in the days of Isaiah and Hosea. He denounced the social sins of his day. (Micah 2:2) He wanted the people to know that every cruel act to one's fellow man was an insult to God. God is offended by the conduct of the people and the rulers.

The Book of Micah seems to be divided into three parts, each beginning with "hear ye." (Micah 1:2; 3:1; 6:1) And each closes with a promise—Micah 2:12,13; 5:10,15; and 7:20.

CHRIST IN MICAH

Birthplace named...........................Micah 5:2
Christ as King............................Micah 2:12,13
Christ reigning in righteousness over
   the whole earth........................Micah 4:1,7

MESSAGE TO THE PEOPLE (Read Micah 1; 2)

The book opens with the cry, *Hear, all ye people; hearken, O earth, and all that therein is: and let the Lord GOD be witness against you* (Micah 1:2).

God is not asleep. He knows the sad condition of His people and He will judge Israel because of their wrongdoings. Captivity and exile are their fate. God rebukes them for social injustice, unfaithfulness, dishonesty, and idolatry. What are their sins? (Micah 2:1-11)

More and more we are realizing the social value of the Gospel of the Lord Jesus Christ. Wherever this Gospel goes we find conditions bettered and a true Christian brotherhood which is based on sonship. Heart worship of God always issues in practical demonstrations of changed lives. Missionaries all bear witness of this in a most wonderful way.

MESSAGE TO THE RULERS (Read Micah 3—5)

Hear . . . O heads of Jacob, and ye princes of the house of Israel (Micah 3:1). What does God say of them? Read Micah 3:1-4. God likens their covetousness and self aggrandizement, even at the price of blood, to cannibalism. The leaders are devouring the poor defenseless people. *Who hate the good, and love the evil; who pluck off their skin from off them, and their flesh from off their bones; who also eat the flesh of my people, and flay their skin from off them; and they break their bones, and chop them in pieces, as for the pot, and as flesh within the caldron* (Micah 3:2,3). Do you wonder God has a case against them?

The nation was ready for a collapse and the princes and priests were responsible for it. God denounces the sin of the rulers (Micah 3:9), the bribery among the judges (Micah 3:11), false weights and balances. "Ye twist all that is straight" are God's words. God describes these men in Micah 3:5. *That make my people err, that bite with their teeth and cry, Peace.*

Micah, broken-hearted, tells of God's judgment upon Judah for their sins. Jerusalem and its temple will be destroyed. (Micah 3:12; 7:13) The people of Judah will be taken captive to Babylon. (Micah 4:10) But he seems to hasten over words of judgment, and to linger over the message of God's love and mercy. God will bring His people back from captivity. (Micah 4:1-8; 7:11,14-17) Micah was a prophet of hope. He always looked beyond doom and punishment to the day of glory when Christ Himself shall reign, when peace shall cover the earth. God gives the promise. The Messiah will come. He will be born in Bethlehem. (Micah 4:8; 5:2-4)

Then Israel will be gathered from the nations into which she has been scattered. (Micah 4:6) O, that the Prince of Peace might come soon and make all these things come to pass. We pray with John on the isle of Patmos, *Even so, come, Lord Jesus* (Rev. 22-20).

GOD'S GOVERNMENT

Jerusalem, capital of Christ's Kingdom . . . . . . **Micah 4:1,2**
Universal extent of Christ's Kingdom . . . . **Micah 4:2**
Peace, keynote of Christ's Kingdom . . . . **Micah 4:3**
Prosperity, blessing of Christ's Kingdom . . . . . . **Micah 4:4**
Righteousness, Basis of Christ's Kingdom . . **Micah 4:5; 4:2**

Little Bethlehem, smallest among the towns of Judah, shall be signally honored by the birth of God's Messiah, Jesus Christ, our Lord. He comes as a little babe to bring salvation to a world so in need of a Redeemer. This seven hundred year old prophecy from Micah 5:2-5 led the wise men to seek the new King.

MESSAGE TO THE CHOSEN PEOPLE
(Read Micah 6–7)

A momentous debate is on between God and His people! *Hear ye, O mountains, the LORD'S controversy, and ye strong foundations of the earth: for the LORD hath a controversy with his people, and he will plead with Israel* (Micah 6:2). God is pictured as one bringing a law-suit against His people. He tells them to remember how good He has been to them and how He has kept His covenant with them. *O my people, what have I done unto thee? and wherein have I wearied thee? testify against me* (Micah 6:3).

The people, conscience-smitten, ask how they can please God. Frantically they ask if burnt-offerings will do. Listen to their cry! *Wherewith shall I come before the LORD, and bow myself before the high God? shall I come before him with burnt-offerings, with calves of a year old? Will the LORD be pleased with thousands of rams, or with ten thousands of rivers of oil? shall I give my firstborn for my transgression, the fruit of my body for the sin of my soul* (Micah 6:6,7)?

Man is always trying to get back in the good graces of God with some outward religious service or some material goods. But remember the *sacrifices of God are a broken spirit: a broken and a contrite heart, O God, thou wilt not despise* (Psalm 51:17). God wants righteous conduct, and a real personal experience of Him in each life. Because of unrighteous conduct the people had to suffer unbelievable consequences. God is a righteous Judge. (Micah 1:3,6; 3:12) What does the apostle Paul tell us to do in return for God's mercies? (Read Rom. 12:1,2.) The best way to get back in God's graces is to accept God's grace.

The Old Testament gives a definition of religion. What does God require of thee?

> Do justly—good ethics in business.
>
> Love kindness—consider others.
>
> Walk humbly with thy God (See Micah 6:8.)

How does this compare with man's present day definitions of "religion"?

We must *worship God in spirit and in truth* (John 4:24). Christ wants us to have more than a beautiful creed even if it is spiritual and Christ-like. He wants this spirit of Christ to be lived out through our daily lives and to be exhibited in our homes, and in our business. Can our religion stand this test?

PROPHECIES FROM MICAH

CHRIST'S BIRTH—Micah 5:2 . . . Micah's chief prophecy centers about Christ. "All the chief priests and scribes of the people," called together by Herod 700 years later, learned from this book the birthplace of Christ.

CHRIST'S RULE—Micah 5:2 . . . declares that Christ was to go forth from Bethlehem as Ruler, even though He arrived there as a babe. This destiny was His from the days of eternity.

CHRIST'S GLORY—Micah 5:4 . . . portrays His kingdom in majesty and ultimate glory. *He shall stand and feed in the strength of the LORD, in the majesty of the name of the LORD his God; and they shall abide: for now shall he be great unto the ends of the earth.*

QUIZ OF OBADIAH, JONAH, MICAH

God's judgment on Edom as Israel's notable enemy should warn nations today that God has *not* cast off His people and that nations that oppress them will surely bring down His judgments. (Read Gen. 12:3.) What nations today have been punished because of their treatment of the Jews?

How is Christ portrayed in Obadiah?

Can you tell the story of Jonah given in three short chapters of the book?

Why is it hard for people to accept this story of Jonah?

That the story of Jonah and the whale is more than a mere fish story is evident in a striking statement of Jesus revealed by the apostle Matthew in his Gospel (12:40).

How is Christ portrayed in Jonah?

Are the sins of Israel, social injustice, faithlessness, dishonesty and idolatry, the sins of America?

Is there social injustice in America? Where?

Is our slogan "In God we trust" true today?

236

Do our business methods show dishonesty?

Do we misrepresent? Are we law breakers?

What other gods does America worship besides the one true God?

What is the social value of the Gospel?

In what chapter and verse does Micah tell of Christ's birth in Bethlehem?

How is Christ portrayed in Micah?

Minimum Daily Requirements / Spiritual Vitamins

Sunday: DOOM AND DELIVERANCE Obadiah 1–21

Monday: A FISH STORY Jonah 1; 2

Tuesday: AN OBEDIENT PROPHET Jonah 3; 4

Wednesday: A MESSAGE TO THE PEOPLE Micah 1; 2

Thursday: A MESSAGE TO THE RULERS Micah 3; 4

Friday: THE BIRTH AND REJECTION OF THE KING
Micah 5

Saturday: A MESSAGE TO THE CHOSEN PEOPLE
Micah 6; 7

Chapter 24

LET'S LOOK AT NAHUM, HABAKKUK, ZEPHANIAH

*JESUS CHRIST, A STRONGHOLD IN
THE DAY OF TROUBLE; THE GOD OF
MY SALVATION; A JEALOUS LORD*

Nahum was written about one hundred fifty years after the revival of Jonah's day when the city of Nineveh was brought to repentance in "dust and ashes." Mercy unheeded finally brings judgment.

No doubt the Ninevites were sincere then, but it did not last. They were guilty of the very sins of which they had repented. Nineveh, the glory of the Assyrians, had come to a complete and deliberate defiance of the living

God. They were not just backsliders! They deliberately rejected the God they had accepted. (II Kings, 18:25,30,35; 19:10-13)

God sent Nahum to predict their final doom and complete overthrow. This empire had been built up by violence. The Assyrians were great warriors. They were out on raiding expeditions continually. They built their state on the loot of other people. Their practices were cruel. They skinned their prisoners alive and dressed columns with their skin, or cut off their hands, feet, noses, ears. They put out their eyes, pulled out their tongues. They burned boys and girls in fire. They made mounds of human skulls. They did everything to inspire terror. They said they did this in obedience to their god, Asshur. God was going to doom them to perish in a violent and extraordinary way. All this came to pass about eighty-six years later. Read of their beast-like violence and cruelty. (Nahum 2:11,12)

THE JUDGE (Read Nahum 1:1-7)

In Nahum 1, we see God, the holy Judge, at the bench of the court of heaven judging the wicked city of Nineveh. The case is presented. This God is a just God, therefore He must avenge all crimes.

Notice God did not bring judgment on Assyria in hot haste. He had been patient for a long time. He is *slow to anger, and plenteous in mercy*. But God sent ruin. He is a God of absolute justice. He is the Lord God, merciful and gracious, long-suffering and forgiving iniquity, yet He will by no means excuse the guilty. Jonah had dwelt on the first side of God's character—love. (Jonah 4:2) Nahum brings out the second—the holiness of God which must deal with sin in judgment. (Nahum 1:2,6)

THE VERDICT OF NINEVEH (Read Nahum 1:8-14)

1. Condemned to destruction....................1:8, 9
2. Captured while drunk........................ 1:10
3. Name blotted out............................ 1:14
4. God to dig her grave........................ 1:14

Nineveh had been weighed in the balance and found wanting.

We cannot read this without being struck by the solemnity of it all. Nahum prophesied this destruction. Today the traveler finds this great city Nineveh of the past still lying in ruins. The Judge has brought everything to pass.

This book gives us the picture of the wrath of God. Read the second verse again, *God is jealous, and the LORD revengeth, and is furious; the LORD will take vengeance on his adversaries, and he reserveth wrath for his enemies.* This is a picture of God acting in wrath. We are living in a day when we make little reference to this truth about God. We only hear of the love of God. But God still is a holy God. He hates sin. He will bring judgment upon it.

THE EXECUTION (Read Nahum 2; 3)

Read what God says in these short chapters. We find a picture of Nineveh's siege, fall and desolation described with graphic eloquence in Nahum 2; 3. All that God can do with a rebellious and defiant nation is to destroy it. Her name should be utterly cut off, and He would dig her grave. The mustering of the armies around Nineveh is pictured in such a way that the prophet makes his hearers see all the horrid sights of the tragic scene.

Outside the walls the Medes gathered. Shields were brilliantly painted. Robes were of purple. Terrible spears glittered in the sun. Knives on their chariot wheels flashed in the light. Inside the city pandemonium reigned! Too late the king tried to rally his drunken nobles to defend the beloved city. But the Tigris had caused a flood which had washed away most of the wall which had seemed to them an impregnable fortress. This aided their enemies. Queen Huzzab was taken captive, and her maidens, like a flock of doves, moaned around her.

The cries of the Medes were heard as they shouted to one another. "Rob ye silver, rob ye gold, for there is no limit to the precious treasures." The city was looted while the people stood with their knees smiting together for fear. Nineveh would no longer terrify the nations because God had made an end of her. This will happen to all wicked nations of the earth.

The Medes and Babylonians completely destroyed Nineveh in 607 B.C. It occurred at the zenith of her power. According to Nahum's prophecy, it came true that a sudden rise of the Tigris, carrying away a great part of the wall, assisted the attacking army of the Medes and Babylonians in its overthrow. (Nahum 2:6) It was partly destroyed by fire. (Nahum 3:13,15)

So deeply and effectively did God dig Nineveh's grave that every trace of its existence disappeared for ages and its site was not known. When Alexander the Great fought the battle of Arbela nearby in 331 B.C., he didn't even know there had ever been a city there. When Xenophon and his army of 10,000 passed by two hundred years later, he thought the mounds were the ruins of some Parthian city. When Napoleon encamped near its site, he, too, was not aware of it.

The city had one denunciation more, given a few years later by Zephaniah. (Zephaniah 2:13) In 607 B.C. the whole was fulfilled.

So complete was the destruction that all traces of the Assyrian Empire disappeared. Many scholars thought the references in the Bible were only mythical. It seemed that no such city ever existed. In 1845, Layard confirmed the suspicions of the Englishman, Claud James Rich, who in 1820 thought the mounds across the Tigris from Mosul were the ruins of Nineveh. The ruins of the magnificent palaces of the Assyrian kings, and thousands of inscriptions were unearthed which give to us the story of Assyria as the Assyrians wrote it themselves. And so the magnificent capital, the wealthiest and most splendid city in the world of its day, has been discovered and the Bible account has been confirmed.

As Nineveh sowed, so must she reap. This is God's law. Nineveh had fortified herself so that nothing could harm her. With walls one hundred feet high and wide enough for four chariots to go abreast, and a circumference of eighty miles, and adorned by hundreds of towers, she sat complacently. A moat one hundred and forty feet wide and sixty feet deep surrounded the vast walls. But Nineveh reckoned without Jehovah. What are bricks and mortar to God! The mighty empire which Shalmaneser, Sargon, and Sennacherib had built up, the Lord threw down with a stroke, and that beyond all recovery. The inventions of civilization are powerless against heaven's artillery.

Nineveh stands for nations that turn their backs from following God. In our day, proud civilizations are staking everything upon the strength of man power and machines and there is an utter disregard of God. We find that Nineveh was overthrown because of her sin (Nahum 3:1-7) and that her great wealth and strength was not sufficient to save her. (Nahum 3:8-19) The person or nation that deliberately and finally rejects God, deliberately and finally and fatally elects doom. Beware of this!

Hear Peter's words of warning spoken hundreds of years later—*The Lord is not slack concerning his promise, as some men count slackness; but is long-suffering to us-ward, not willing that any should perish, but that all should come to repentance. But the day of the Lord will come as a thief in the night; in the which the heavens shall pass away with a great noise, and the elements shall melt with fervent heat, the earth also and the works that are therein shall be burned up* (II Peter 3:9,10).

THE BOOK OF HABAKKUK

HABAKKUK'S COMPLAINT (Read Habakkuk 1)

This scene opens with the cry of a man who has a problem he cannot solve. *O LORD, how long shall I cry, and thou wilt not hear* (1:1-4)! Habakkuk was confused and bewildered. It seemed to him that God was doing nothing to straighten out the conditions in the world. He had lived during the days of the great reformation under the good King Josiah. He had seen Assyria fading in power and Babylon, under Nebuchadnezzar, rising to a place of supremacy. The world about him was in an upheaval. Violence abounded and God was doing nothing about it.

But worse than all, he saw his own land, Judah, full of lawlessness and tyranny. The righteous were oppressed. (Hab. 1:2,13) The people were living in open sin. (Hab. 2:4,5,15,16) They were worshiping idols. (Hab. 2:18,19) They were oppressing the poor. (Hab. 1:4,14,15) Habakkuk knew that the day was dark. He knew that this sin was leading to an invasion of Jerusalem by a strong enemy.

Habakkuk asked his question of God. He didn't call a committee or form a society to solve the problem of the day. He went straight to Jehovah and stated his problem. Then we hear God answering, *I will work a work in your days, which ye will not believe, though it be told you* (Hab. 1:5). God tells Habakkuk that He is not indifferent to His people. He wants Habakkuk to look beyond the present. He is already working. God has called the Chaldeans to the work of punishing Judah. They are a cruel scourge which will sweep over the land to destroy it. (Hab. 1:5-11)

God's answer seems to horrify Habakkuk. He cannot understand how God would allow such an enemy to punish His own people when He Himself is so pure and holy. Habakkuk challenges God to defend His actions. (Hab. 1:13)

The nations have always been God's object lessons, illustrating His moral laws. (Hab. 1:12)

GOD'S REPLY (Read Habakkuk 2)

Here we see Habakkuk facing the great moment of his life. Watch him as he climbs upon the watchtower to wait for God. He expects God to answer him. He turns his face toward heaven and thinks, "I will wait and see what this is all about." *I will stand upon my watch, and set me upon the tower, and will watch to see what he will say unto me, and what I shall answer when I am reproved* (Hab. 2:1).

Everything lies in ruins around the prophet. Chaldea is coming up to destroy what is left. There is only One to whom he can turn, so he waits expectantly for God. God gives an answer. (Hab. 2:2-20) God admits the wickedness of the Chaldeans, but declares that they will destroy themselves finally by their own evil. Pride and cruelty always bring destruction. Men sometimes have to wait to know what the final outcome will be. God sometimes takes the ages to show His plans. *One day is with the Lord as a thousand years, and a thousand years as one day* (II Peter 3:8). God's testing always reveals what men are. He burns out the dross. It may

244

seem that the Chaldeans are prospering for a time but they are doomed.

HABAKKUK'S SONG (Read Habakkuk 3)

Habakkuk is the prophet who sang in the night. Read the wonderful melody with which his prophecy closes. (Hab. 3:17,18) This ode was set to music and sung at the public worship by the Jews.

After a sincere prayer (Hab. 3:1-16) God's glory appears. God always responds to the cry for help from His people. Habakkuk realizes that God is in control of this universe and that He is working out His own purpose in His own time. (Read Rom. 8:28.) Habakkuk learned that he could trust implicitly in God. He realizes that he can see only a small part of God's plan at one time. One must wait for God to reveal His entire program.

Most of us are like a small boy watching a parade through a knothole in the fence. All he can see is just what is passing before him. But his friend who has climbed a telegraph pole nearby is throwing his cap in the air and shouting because he can see the elephants coming and the entire parade. His friend below sees nothing yet. He can't imagine what the fellow above him is shouting about. God's prophets are men whom God has lifted to high watchtowers and has shown to them events that are coming long before they happen. The people below only see what is taking place before their very eyes at the moment it happens, as the boy peeking through the knothole.

One of the texts in Habakkuk is quoted three times in the New Testament. It has great significance in the history of the Reformation. Do you know the story of the young monk, Martin Luther, who rose to his feet as he was crawling up the Sancta Scala in Rome? He remembered these words, *The just shall live by his faith* (Hab. 2:4). Not by works! This started him out on his great crusade which brought about the Reformation.

THE BOOK OF ZEPHANIAH

Zephaniah held the torch high to light up Judah's wickedness and idolatry. Such a man disturbs this old world in its sins. They call him a troublemaker, a meddler, and try to silence him. But if it were not for the word of the prophet in the evil day, the world would soon slide into a pit of vice. Think of Luther and his fearless voice in the midst of the dark days that preceded the Reformation. Let sin go on and it will destroy any civilization. *Righteousness exalteth a nation: but sin is a reproach to any people* (Proverbs 14:34).

THE NATIONS SEARCHED (Read Zephaniah 1; 2)

Jehovah is in the midst of the land for judgment. (See Zeph. 3:5 and 1:17.) He first searches Judah and pronounces doom on all those who are worshiping idols. The land must be freed from idolatry. Jehovah cannot allow such abomination to remain. We see the rulers are denounced as is every class of sinner. (Zeph. 1:7-13)

The prophet calls the people to seek God (Zeph. 2:1-3) that they may be hid in the day of the Lord's wrath. He declares that nothing can save the nation from doom but real repentance. *Seek ye the Lord . . . seek righteousness, seek meekness* is his admonition.

Then he turns to the five heathen nations, Philistia, Moab, Ammon, Ethiopia and Assyria. They shall be visited with the wrath of God because of their pride and scorn toward the Lord's people. (Zeph. 2:10)

ISRAEL RESTORED (Read Zephaniah 3)

The prophet concludes with the most wonderful promises of Israel's future restoration and of the happy state of the purified people of God in the latter days. (Zeph. 3) The redeemed remnant will return cleansed, humbled, trusting and rejoicing with their offerings to Zion. They will be established in their land with God "in their midst." (Zeph. 3:15,17) Zion then shall be a delight among nations and a blessing to the whole earth as was foretold in the promise God made originally with Abraham. (See Gen. 12:1-3)

The rejoicing of Zeph. 3:14-20 must refer to something beside the day when the remnant will return after the captivity of Babylon. Judah's worst judgment followed that return. She has seen little but misery ever since. Neither did anything like this occur at Christ's first coming. It must refer to the day when the Lord Himself shall sit on the throne of David, when His people shall be gathered from the four corners of the earth. (Zeph. 3:19) This prophecy shall be blessedly fulfilled in the kingdom age when Christ comes to this earth to reign in power and great glory.

QUIZ OF NAHUM, HABAKKUK, ZEPHANIAH

How is Christ portrayed in Nahum?

Why was God allowing sin to go on unchecked? Why didn't God stop the lawless and godless ones from plunging the whole world into despair and doom? Aren't we asking God similar questions in the hour in which we are living? It is difficult sometimes to understand God's ways. You cannot always judge a man by his acts. You must know him to understand why he is doing as he is.

God has an answer to every problem in life. We must learn to take our place and wait for God to reveal it to us.

Did God give Habakkuk an answer? What did the prophet learn about waiting for God to answer?

Mark Reformat on text in your Bible.

Find where Habakkuk 2:4 is quoted in the New Testament: Rom. 1:17; Gal. 3:11; Heb. 10:38. (Mark them.)

How is Christ portrayed in Habakkuk?

What is the promise of hope given to Israel by the minor prophets? When will this promise be fulfilled?

How is Christ portrayed in Zephaniah?

Minimum Daily Requirements / Spiritual Vitamins

Sunday: THE JUDGE AND THE VERDICT Nahum 1

Monday: THE EXECUTION Nahum 2; 3

Tuesday: HABAKKUK'S COMPLAINT Habakkuk 1

Wednesday: GOD'S REPLY Habakkuk 2

Thursday: HABAKKUK'S SONG Habakkuk 3

Friday: COMING JUDGMENTS Zephaniah 1; 2

Saturday: THE KINGDOM BLESSINGS Zephaniah 3

Chapter 25

LET'S LOOK AT HAGGAI, ZECHARIAH, MALACHI

JESUS CHRIST, THE DESIRE OF ALL NATIONS; THE RIGHTEOUS BRANCH; SUN OF RIGHTEOUSNESS

The greater number of the Old Testament prophets spoke before the captivity. During the captivity, Ezekiel and Daniel prophesied. After the return Haggai, Zechariah and Malachi prophesied. This makes it easy for you to remember. Just two during the exile, three after, then all of the other twelve of the seventeen before. Learn these facts now!

Haggai, Zechariah and Malachi are the last of the prophetic books. Each of these prophets belongs to the period after the exile. They prophesied to the Jews after they had returned to Jerusalem.

A MESSAGE OF REBUKE (Read Haggai 1:1-11)

Many of the exiles that had returned from Babylon had become more interested in building homes for themselves then rebuilding the temple. They left it in ruins. They definitely put self first and God last. (Hag. 1:4) God would not allow this to go on and so He sent punishment as a result. Poor crops, droughts, failing trade, misery and turmoil made their spirits fail. They were working and slaving but finding no real joy. (Hag. 1:6,9-11)

Haggai's stern call to duty proved to be a good tonic. Zerubbabel, the governor of Jerusalem, Joshua, the high priest, and the people arose and began the work of rebuilding the temple. (Hag. 1:12-15) How did God respond to their repentance? (Hag. 1:13)

God sometimes allows hardships because of our indifference to Him. Crops had failed and business was depressed because of the sin of the Jews. But God wants us to keep up the church. Without churches sin and vice will grow. When men forget to love God, they forget to love their fellow men, too. We should beautify God's house. (See II Sam. 7:2) We are not to live in fine homes and allow God's house to be in ruins.

Does Haggai 1:6 describe the modern wage earner's purse?

A MESSAGE OF COURAGE (Read Haggai 2:1-9)

How long after the first message was this one given? (Hag. 1:1; 2:1) For the history of this period read Ezra 3:8-13.

As the people were building, a new discouragement seized them. The older ones remembering the splendor of the temple of Solomon were greatly disappointed in this new temple. It did not measure up in any way, they thought. How inferior in size and costliness of the stones! How much smaller in extent was the foundation itself! How limited were their means. And besides, this second temple would not have the things that made the first one so glorious—the ark, the Shekinah, and all that went with the service of the high priest. These pessimists dampened the enthusiasm of the builders.

But Haggai came with a word of cheer. God was to pour His resources into that new building. The living God was to be in the midst of this new temple. *The desire of all nations shall come: and I will fill this house with glory, saith the LORD of hosts* (Hag. 2:7). Jesus stood in the temple of His day five hundred years later. He drove out the traders and worked His miracles in its precincts. He filled the temple with the glory of God.

A MESSAGE OF ASSURANCE (Read Haggai 2:10–23)

This message of cleansing and blessing was delivered three months after the temple was started. Haggai heard their complaints of seeing no visible signs of blessings although they had been working for full three months. Haggai showed them that the land had been rendered useless by their neglect but God was working and it would be different now. *From this day will I bless you.* (Read Hag. 2:18,19.) God begins when we begin. Zechariah, no doubt, was preaching with Haggai these days. God sometimes withholds prosperity of wealth to give prosperity of soul.

Some pertinent lessons from Haggai:

Undertake great things for God and you will not be alone.

Give God at least that which is as good as you give yourself.

Build for God. Dr. George Lorimer used to say that

every man should leave behind him something that lasts.

THE BOOK OF ZECHARIAH

THE CHOSEN PEOPLE AND THE TEMPLE
(Read Zechariah 1–8)

Sixteen years had passed since the first exiles had returned to Jerusalem, and still there was no temple. The Gentile nations were at peace and now was the time to build. (See Zech. 1:14-16.) Zechariah warned the people not to disappoint God as their fathers had done. He quickened their hopes by painting in glowing colors a picture of God's love and the time of perpetual blessing that was coming to Israel in the far off ages. He pictures Utopia where everyone would sit under his own "vine and fig tree."

THE KING COMETH!

Zechariah foretells the Saviour more than any other prophet save Isaiah.

Haggai told the Jews of a day when a house far greater and more glorious than the great temple of

Solomon would be built by a Descendant of Zerubbabel with the treasures from "all nations." (See Hag. 2:7-9.) This Descendant of Zerubbabel would be the Branch that would come out of David's household. The house He would build would be a spiritual house, built on the doctrine of grace, by the Holy Spirit of God. (Read Zech. 4:6-9; 6:12,13.)

Zechariah, looking far into the future, saw the Messiah coming first in humiliation and suffering, and again, in majesty and great glory. The Jew ignores the Christ of the cross, coming in humiliation. The Christian, too often, ignores the Christ of the crown, coming in glory. Which is worse?

Zechariah seems to let the glory of Christ glow in all his teaching and preaching. (See "Visions of Zechariah.")

VISIONS OF ZECHARIAH

Of the Minor Prophets, Zechariah alone majors in visions. "I saw by night and behold . . ." (1:7,8)

The Angelic Horsemen (1:7-17) A picture of Israel today, outcast, but not forgotten by God.

The Horns and Smiths (1:18-21) The overthrow of Israel by her enemies is foreseen.

The Measuring Line (2) The coming prosperity of Jerusalem, walled in by the presence of God.

Joshua, the High Priest (3) Filthy garments, clothing priest, and representing Israel's sin, are removed, replaced, and the Branch, Christ, introduced.

The Golden Candlesticks (4) Israel is shown as God's future lightbearer. Olive trees, anointed of God, speak of Zerubbabel, the ruler, and Joshua, the priest.

The Flying Roll (5:1-4) Wicked governments receive God's curse in this unique picture.

The Ephah (5:5-11) Borne away on divine wings, wickedness is removed.

The Four Chariots (6:1-8) "Administrative forces of righteousness"—Dr. G. Campbell Morgan.

THE MESSIAH AND THE KINGDOM
(Read Zechariah 9—14)

This scene is full of promises of the coming Messiah and a world-wide kingdom. The prophet pictures no longer a city rebuilt on its old foundations, but a glorious city whose wall is the Lord. It is not armed for war, but is a city filled with peace for the Prince of Peace reigns. This great Prince shall come the first time as the lowly One riding upon a humble beast used by kings on errands of peace. (Read Zech. 9:9.)

But we see this lowly One becoming a mighty Sovereign. (Zech. 14:8-11) The conflict of the ages will cease and a glorious victory will be the ultimate. The Messiah in all His glory and might shall put all enemies under His feet and He shall establish His kingdom in Jerusalem and sit upon the throne of David. *His dominion shall be from sea even to sea, and from the river even to the ends of the earth* (Zech. 9:10).

THE BOOK OF MALACHI

By this time, a hundred years or more had passed since the Jews had returned to Jerusalem after the captivity in Babylon. Malachi is the last prophet to speak to Israel in her own land. Israel here means all the remnant of Israel and Judah that returned after the exile. The first enthusiasm after the return from Babylon had spent itself. Following a period of revival (Neh. 10:28-39), the people had become cold religiously and lax morally.

The prophet Malachi came as a reformer, but he encouraged while he rebuked. He dealt with a people perplexed, with spirits failing, whose faith in God seemed to be in danger of collapse. If they had not already become hostile to Jehovah, they were in real danger of becoming skeptical.

Malachi means "the messenger of the Lord." Like the forerunner, John the Baptist, of whom he prophesies, he was but a voice.

THE SINS OF THE PRIESTS (Read Malachi 1:1–2:9)

God's condemnation begins with the leaders. (Mal. 2:1-9) As long as the priests were openly unfit, what could be expected from the people at large? This resulted in a carelessness among God's people in keeping themselves separate from the heathen nations. Mixed marriages with women of outside tribes became common. Some men had not hesitated to divorce their Israelitish wives to make this possible. (Mal. 2:10-16)

The priests became irreverent and neglectful. Read Malachi 1:6,11,12. God said, *Where is mine honor? . . . O priests, that despise my name.* The prophet rebuked these careless priests for offering worthless animals in sacrifice to God that they would not offer to the governor. (Mal. 1:7,8,12,13) They stood in marked contrast to God's ideal for the priesthood. (Mal. 2:4-11) They had completely lost sight of their high calling and deserved the ignominy heaped upon them. They refused to work except for money.

THE SINS OF THE PEOPLE (Read Malachi 2:10–3:18)

What would you think of a person who deliberately held something before his eyes and then complained that he could see nothing? What would you suggest might quickly solve the difficulty? Well, this is just what Malachi had to do. The Jews declared that Jehovah did not love them as He said. (Mal. 1:2) They could not see that His love had been of any special advantage to them.

These sins which were blinding Israel's eyes may be blinding ours. Let us learn what they are.

These were the sins which Malachi rebuked. Are they yours, too? Suppose we do find some of these sins in our daily lives, what are we to do? Confess them to Jehovah. Israel was troubled about the result of her confession. Malachi had to encourage the people by assuring them of Jehovah's wonderful love and giving the beautiful promise of Malachi 3:7. Turn to it and mark it in your Bible.

The children of Israel could depend on Jehovah to forgive. It was this same picture of the Father that Jesus gave when He told of the prodigal's return. The father, seeing the boy while yet a great way off, *ran* out to meet him. This is God's attitude. Turn to I John 1:9 and read this for your own confession.

The Jews had been cured of idolatry, but they had grown careless and indifferent about many things. They had neglected the house of God. The priests had become lax. They were bringing inferior sacrifices to the temple. They had robbed God of their tithes and offerings. They fell into social sins. They had become so selfish and covetous that Malachi dared to challenge them with these words, "Will a man rob God?" (Mal. 3:8)

The key that opens God's big blessing windows is your recognition of His ownership by giving back to Him a proper share of the money or the property that He permits you to acquire. *Bring ye all the tithes into the storehouse.* The tenth (or tithe) is the outward recognition that everything belongs to God. We are to bring Him our whole selves, body, soul and spirit. Then He will accept us and open the windows of heaven to pour out His blessings.

If you will take the trouble to investigate, you will find that many men of big business have found great happiness and great prosperity by this key. John Wanamaker was a tither from his youth. Colgate, of soap fame, as a boy, gave to God a dime out of the first dollar he ever earned. He became a multi-millionaire. A. A. Hyde of Mentholatum fame says he began tithing when he was 100,000 dollars in debt. Many men have said they consider it dishonest to give God one tenth of their incomes while they were in debt. Mr. Hyde said he thought that way until one day it flashed upon him that God was his first creditor. When he began paying God back first, all the other creditors were eventually paid, too.

COMING THINGS (Read Malachi 3; 4)

What's the use of being good? Is this not one of the standing complaints of those who think they are good men? They say, "What is God doing that He permits such things?" The answer to such a complaint is that Jehovah does care. He showed this to them by saying that one day He will send His messenger (John the Baptist) to prepare His way. Then He will come in person "suddenly" and sit in judgment and separate the evil from the good. (Mal. 3:1) His judgment will be searching and effective "like a refiner's fire," like "fullers' soap." (Mal. 3:2,3) When God really gets ready to act, what will He do? (Mal. 3:1-3) The action will be final!

LEARN MALACHI THIS WAY

The attitude of the people is exhibited in six "WHEREINS."
Mark them in your Bible.

1. God says, . . . "I have loved you."
   Israel says, . . . "Wherein hast Thou loved us?" (1:2)

2. God says, . . . "Ye despise My name."
   Israel says, . . . "Wherein have we despised Thy name?" (1:6)

3. God says, . . . "Ye offer polluted bread upon mine altar."
   Israel says, . . . "Wherein have we polluted Thee?" (1:7)

4. God says, . . . "Ye have wearied the Lord with your words."
   Israel says, . . . "Wherein have we wearied Him?" (2:17)

5. God says, . . . "Return unto Me."
   Israel says, . . . "Wherein shall we return?" (3:7)

6. God says, . . . "Ye have robbed me."
   Israel says, . . . "Wherein have we robbed Thee?" (3:8)

Two "whats" may be added:

   "What have we spoken so much against Thee?" (3:13)
   "What profit is it that we have kept His ordinances?" (3:14)

Oh, how we need God's Malachi today to be sent before Him, to prepare His way so that God's people may honor and adore Him. Malachi cries, "Back to God's house! Back to God's Word! Back to God's work! Back to God's grace!"

Malachi is the last prophet of the Old Testament. Four hundred years were to elapse before another prophet, John the Baptist, would speak for God. John broke the silence by his thrilling message that God had become flesh; that He was dwelling in our midst, and that we could behold His glory!

QUIZ OF HAGGAI, ZECHARIAH, MALACHI

How did Haggai state the common admonition "Watch your step"? (1:5)

Did you ever hear a person say that his pockets had holes? This is as old as Haggai. (520 B.C.) (See 1:6.)

Who is the "desire of all nations"? (2:7)

How is Christ portrayed in Haggai?

Tell about the Utopia described in Zech. 3:10.

What two sins are mentioned in Zech. 5:3? Are these common today?

In Zech. 9:9 you have Palm Sunday described. Find it.

The desire of the peoples of the earth today is "one world." When will this be true? (See Zech. 9:9)

Can you recall five prophecies foretold in Zechariah?

Recall three visions of Zechariah.

How is Christ portrayed in Zechariah?

What sins does God lay to the charge of the people in Malachi?

How does God say we may "prove" Him? (Mal. 3:10)

Name some men who have proved God this way.

How is Christ portrayed in Malachi?

Minimum Daily Requirements / Spiritual Vitamins

Sunday: HAGGAI'S MESSAGE Haggai 1; 2
Monday: VISIONS Zechariah 1–6
Tuesday: FASTS Zechariah 7; 8
Wednesday: RESTORATION OF JUDAH AND ISRAEL
           Zech. 9–11
Thursday: THE MESSIAH Zechariah 12–14
Friday: SINS OF PRIESTS AND PEOPLE Malachi 1; 2
Saturday: MESSAGE OF HOPE Malachi 3; 4

Chapter 26

A QUICK LOOK AT THE OLD TESTAMENT

ESTHER THROUGH MALACHI

ESTHER

THEME OF BOOK: Jesus Christ is portrayed as our Advocate.

OUTSTANDING LESSON: God will deliver His children!

JOB

THEME OF BOOK: Jesus Christ is portrayed as our Redeemer.

OUTSTANDING LESSON: Why do the righteous suffer?

PSALMS

THEME OF BOOK: Jesus Christ is portrayed as our All in All.

OUTSTANDING LESSON: Praise God!

PROVERBS

THEME OF BOOK: Jesus Christ is portrayed as the End of all living.

OUTSTANDING LESSON: Get wisdom!

ECCLESIASTES

THEME OF BOOK: Jesus Christ is portrayed as the End of all living.

OUTSTANDING LESSON: Try wisdom!

SONG OF SOLOMON

THEME OF BOOK: Jesus Christ is portrayed as the Lover of our souls.

OUTSTANDING LESSON: Love God!

ISAIAH

THEME OF BOOK: Jesus Christ is portrayed as the Messiah.

OUTSTANDING LESSON: Salvation is of God!

JEREMIAH

THEME OF BOOK: Jesus Christ is portrayed as the Righteous Branch.

OUTSTANDING LESSON: Go and tell!

LAMENTATIONS

THEME OF BOOK: Jesus Christ is portrayed as the Righteous Branch.

OUTSTANDING LESSON: God's grace always shines!

EZEKIEL

THEME OF BOOK: Jesus Christ is portrayed as the Son of man.

OUTSTANDING LESSON: See visions!

DANIEL

THEME OF BOOK: Jesus Christ is portrayed as the Smiting Stone.

OUTSTANDING LESSON: God is Sovereign!

HOSEA

THEME OF BOOK: Jesus Christ is portrayed as the Healer of the backslider.

OUTSTANDING LESSON: Return unto God!

JOEL

THEME OF BOOK: Jesus Christ is portrayed as the Restorer.

OUTSTANDING LESSON: Repent for "the day of the Lord" cometh.

AMOS

THEME OF BOOK: Jesus Christ is portrayed as the Heavenly Husbandman.

OUTSTANDING LESSON: Prepare to meet thy God!

OBADIAH

THEME OF BOOK: Jesus Christ is portrayed as our Saviour.

OUTSTANDING LESSON: Possess your possessions!

JONAH

THEME OF BOOK: Jesus Christ is portrayed as our Resurrection and Life.

OUTSTANDING LESSON: Arise and go!

MICAH

THEME OF BOOK: Jesus Christ is portrayed as a Witness against rebellious nations.

OUTSTANDING LESSON: Hear ye!

NAHUM

THEME OF BOOK: Jesus Christ is portrayed as a Stronghold in the day of trouble.

OUTSTANDING LESSON: Beware, the Lord avengeth!

HABAKKUK

THEME OF BOOK: Jesus Christ is portrayed as the God of our salvation.

OUTSTANDING LESSON: Live by faith!

ZEPHANIAH

THEME OF BOOK: Jesus Christ is portrayed as a Jealous Lord.

OUTSTANDING LESSON: God is mighty to save!

HAGGAI

THEME OF BOOK: Jesus Christ is portrayed as the Desire of all nations.

OUTSTANDING LESSON: Build for God!

ZECHARIAH

THEME OF BOOK: Jesus Christ is portrayed as the Righteous Branch.

OUTSTANDING LESSON: Turn ye!

MALACHI

THEME OF BOOK: Jesus Christ is portrayed as the Sun of Righteousness.

OUTSTANDING LESSON: Repent and return!